From the Golf Course to the Main Course

· · · · · · · · · · ·

A Cookbook
For Golfers

Greg Parker & Rob Foster

Illustrations By
Dan Malstrom

PARSTAR PUBLICATIONS

From the Golf Course to the Main Course
by
Greg Parker & Rob Foster

First Printing – October 1994

Copyright © 1994 by
Parstar Publications, a division of 1080836 Ontario Inc.
4579 Cedarbrook Lane
Beamsville, Ontario
L0R 1B5

Canadian Cataloguing in Publication Data
Parker, Greg, 1948 –
From the golf course to the main course

Includes index.
ISBN 1-895292-46-8

1. Cookery.   2. Golf – Anecdotes.   I. Foster, Rob,
1959-   II. Title.
TX714.P37 1994   641.5   C94-920244-4

Photography by:
Patricia Holdsworth
Patricia Holdsworth Photography
Regina, Saskatchewan

Dishes and Accessories courtesy of:
Sharawaggi Imports
Regina, Saskatchewan

Golf clubs, clothing and accessories courtesy of:
RAM GOLF CANADA
Wascana Golf Club, Regina, Saskatchewan

Designed, Printed and Produced in Canada by
Centax, Books, A Division of PrintWest Communications
Publishing Director, Photo Designer and Food Stylist – Margo Embury
1150 Eighth Avenue, Regina, Saskatchewan,
Canada   S4R 1C9
(306) 525-2304   Fax (306) 757-2439

2

Table Of Contents

* Recipes have been tested in U.S. Standard measurements. Common metric measurements are given as a convenience for those who are more familiar with metric. Recipes have not been tested in metric.

Ode to a Duffer

I aimed the club
   towards the spot
Rats – I can't believe
   I missed that shot

I topped the ball
   pulled up my head
I knew the fault
   my face turned red

The game of golf
   I love it so
It humbles me,
   it makes me grow

No one saw – hey,
   this is great
how to score –
   a seven or eight?

Two Simple Rules:
On the golf course, always strive to score below par.
In the kitchen, always strive to be rated above par.
Wouldn't life be great if both were achieved!

4

Introduction

Although it was only mid-October, an early frost meant this would be our final golf game of the season. Making the turn to the back nine, we noticed the halfway house was boarded up for the winter, unable to serve another stale sandwich or dry hamburger. Golfers deserve better than this. Since it would be six months before the scent of freshly cut grass and a beautiful day would awaken us from a winter hibernation, we decided to put our off-season time to good use.

Competition on the golf course would make way for our challenge match in the kitchen. Whose greens had more garlic, whose hooks were too fishy, whose birdies would fly, which hot rounds were memorable and which mulligans begged for a second try?

To combine our labors with our loves, we chose to document in a cookbook our love of good food, by preparing interesting and delicious meals for our wives. After all, they had earned a well-deserved break from the kitchen. In writing this book, we've chosen not just the best of our efforts, but also recipes that were simple, exciting or simply an interesting departure from more standard fare.

We hope other golfers will enjoy this book as much as we enjoyed writing it. So here it is, *From the Golf Course to the Main Course ... A Cookbook for Golfers*. We welcome your comments.

Greg Parker and Rob Foster

Acknowledgements

First and foremost, we offer our heartfelt thanks to our wives, Debbie Parker and Sue Foster. We appreciate their patience, their laughter, and their constructive criticism, not to mention several of the best recipes in the book. And we admire their tolerance as they watched us gain 15 pounds tasting these foods, hoping we would lose it all when we were back on the course in the summer.

We would like to thank Margo Embury for her guidance and support with this project. Her suggestions and critiques have been highly appreciated.

We owe thanks to RAM GOLF CANADA for providing us with suitable clothing and equipment for our photography.

And there are many other people deserving our thanks. For all those who have invested time, suggestions and money in this venture, we thank you for trusting us and helping make it all come together.

1. The Practice Tee
(*Appetizers*)

Just as every golf game should have a gentle beginning with a bucket of balls on the practice tee, so every meal should be introduced with hors d'oeuvres. This French term literally translates to "outside the work" so use the practice tee to loosen up and rid yourself of thoughts other than golf. Use these appetizers to excite the tastebuds, tantalizing the brain with culinary delights and anticipation for what follows.

Charlie's Cherry Tomatoes, Spicy and Stuffed

3/4 cup	softened cream cheese	175 mL
1 tbsp.	olive oil	15 mL
1/4 cup	chopped fresh parsley	60 mL
1	garlic clove, minced	1
1 tsp.	chopped fresh dill	5 mL
2 dashes	salt	2 dashes
1 pinch	cayenne pepper	1 pinch
24	cherry tomatoes	24

Soften cream cheese by beating oil into it with a fork. Next, blend parsley, minced garlic, chopped dill, salt and cayenne into cheese. In bottom of cherry tomatoes, make 2 slices in a "+" shape, not all the way through. Scoop out all the seeds. Spoon cheese mixture into tomatoes and refrigerate to harden filling.

Makes 24 appetizers.

Recipe pictured opposite page 16.

Pro's Tip:
To place the filling in the tomatoes, use a pastry bag to create a swirl through to the top.

Definition of Ace:
A World War I flying hero. Also a hole in one. If made, one has the legal right to brag about the shot with all friends, relatives, acquaintances, and strangers every day for the rest of one's life. May also be inscribed on tombstone.

Gary's Cheese
and Salmon Log

2 cups	softened cream cheese	500 mL
7 1/2 oz.	can salmon, drained, bones and skin removed	225 g
dash	Worcestershire sauce	dash
1 tbsp.	chopped Spanish onion	15 mL
3 tbsp.	sherry or sweet white wine	45 mL
4 oz.	pecans or walnuts, finely chopped	115 g
2 tbsp.	Parmesan cheese	30 mL
1/2 cup	finely chopped parsley	125 mL

In a bowl, thoroughly mix the cream cheese, salmon, Worcestershire sauce, onion and wine. Refrigerate at least 30 minutes to set. Mix the chopped nuts, Parmesan cheese and parsley. Spread nut mixture onto a 12" (30 cm) square of waxed paper. To create log, take the salmon and cheese mixture and roll out into a log shape on the waxed paper, coating with parsley and nuts. Set the log on a serving plate and surround with crackers. If not serving immediately, refrigerate the log for up to a day. Remove from the refrigerator 1 hour before serving.

Serves 8.

Rumor put to rest:
Kirk Douglas did not design the first modern golf ball.

Sam's Scrumptious Shrimp Boats

1 cup	softened cream cheese	250 mL
1/2 cup	mayonnaise	125 mL
3	small Belgian endives	3
1/2 cup	ketchup	125 mL
2 tsp.	horseradish	10 mL
dash	Worcestershire sauce	dash
1/4 lb.	small cooked shrimp	115 g

Combine cream cheese and mayonnaise in a bowl, blending until smooth. Spread or pipe mixture into separated, washed and dried endive leaves, leaving a slight hollow running lengthwise. Mix ketchup, horseradish and Worcestershire sauce and spoon or pipe it into the hollow of the cheese in each endive leaf. Arrange shrimp along the top of each stuffed leaf. Refrigerate until ready to serve.

Makes about 24 appetizers.

Recipe pictured opposite page 16.

Pro's Tip:
Make the sauce a few hours ahead to allow the horseradish to spice up the cocktail sauce a little. If endive is not available, substitute inner leaves of Chinese cabbage or romaine lettuce.

How to rattle your opponent:
Ask him how work is going.

Paul's Stuffed Mushroom Caps

15	large mushrooms	15
6 1/2 oz.	can tuna, drained	184 g
2/3 cup	mayonnaise	150 mL
4 tbsp.	grated Parmesan cheese	60 mL
4 tbsp.	oat bran or dried bread crumbs	60 mL
1 tsp.	finely chopped pimiento	5 mL
1	garlic clove, minced	1
1 tsp.	minced onion	5 mL
1 tsp.	lemon juice	5 mL

Remove stems from the mushrooms. Finely chop the stems and place in a mixing bowl. Combine with the remaining ingredients and mix until well blended. Before spooning the tuna mixture into the caps, it is best to cook the round side of the mushrooms. Place the caps with their rounded side up on a broiler pan and broil for 5 minutes, or until slightly browned. Turn over the caps and fill with the blended mixture. Return caps to broiler and continue cooking for another 5 minutes, or until they are lightly browned.

Makes 15 appetizers.

Pro's Tip:
As an alternative, stuff the mushroom caps with escargot. Open a 7 oz. (200 g) tin of snails, drain the juice and wash away any sand or grit. In a frying pan, sauté the snails in 1/4 cup (60 mL) of butter, 1 clove of minced garlic and 1 tbsp. (15 mL) of parsley flakes. Cook and stuff as outlined above. When filling the caps with the mixture, top off with a few drops of garlic butter.

Byron's Bacon, Onion and Olive Tarts

1/2 cup	cottage cheese	125 mL
1 tbsp.	all-purpose flour	45 mL
3 tbsp.	olive oil	45 mL
	salt and pepper, to taste	
1/2 cup	sour cream	125 mL
10 slices	bacon, cut into small pieces	10 slices
1	Spanish onion, diced	1
14 oz. pkg.	frozen puff pastry, thawed	411 g pkg.
1/4 cup	finely chopped stuffed green olives	60 mL

In a food processor, process the cottage cheese until smooth. Add flour, 2 tbsp. (30 mL) oil, salt, pepper and sour cream. Process again until thoroughly mixed. In a skillet, heat remaining oil; add bacon and onions. Sauté until the onions are slightly limp and the bacon slightly cooked (do not cook completely). Lay out the puff pastry and roll until very thin. Cut 4 circles, each 6" (15 cm), from the pastry and place on a baking sheet. Using a spoon, spread the processed mixture evenly over the 4 pastry circles (leave a little pastry showing at the edges). Add the bacon and onion mixture evenly over the top. Finally, sprinkle with the chopped olives. In a preheated oven, bake the tarts for 15 minutes at 425°F (220°C). Cut each circle into 4 wedges, then serve.

Makes 16 appetizers.

*It's **as easy** to lower your handicap as it is to lower your weight in the off-season.*

12

2. Sandtraps
(Shellfish)

The sand shot is unique in that to properly execute it, the club strikes the sand only. The concussion actually lifts the ball into the air, as if on a pillow. Similarly, shellfish often do not derive their flavor and appeal from the meat itself, but from the assorted sauces and seasonings that enhance the flavor of these delicate seafoods.

Pearl's Oysters Surprise

24	oysters	24
24	small snails	24
2	scallions or small white onions, finely chopped	2
2 tbsp.	butter	30 mL
dash	garlic powder (optional) pepper, to taste	dash

After removing the oysters from their shells, mix them with the snails, scallions, butter, garlic powder and pepper. Return the mixture to the oyster shells and cook for 3-4 minutes in a preheated 400°F (200°C) oven. Remove from oven and serve immediately.

Serves 4-6.

Definition of a Sandbagger:
A golfer who wilfully chooses not to submit his lower scores into the compiling of his handicap, to artificially increase it. He thereby gains an unfair advantage in tournaments or competitions with other golfers. Easily spotted using a pencil with an eraser for keeping score.

Missy's Mussels

1 cup	dry white wine	250 mL
3 tbsp.	butter	45 mL
1	medium onion, diced	1
2 tbsp.	finely chopped red sweet pepper	30 mL
2	garlic cloves, minced	2
20	mussels, well scrubbed, alive	20
2 tbsp.	chopped fresh parsley	30 mL

In a large saucepan, combine the wine, butter, onions, sweet pepper and garlic; heat mixture to a boil. Immediately add all the mussels and cover the saucepan. Cook for about 3 minutes, until all the mussels have opened. Remove any mussels that remain closed. Divide the mussels into 2 bowls and pour the stock from the saucepan over each bowl. Sprinkle chopped parsley over each bowl and serve immediately.

Serves 2.

Recipe pictured opposite page 16.

Important points to remember about golf carts:
Never drive them onto greens, into sand traps, through water hazards, over your opponent's ball or over your opponent.

Pam's Clams:
Broil, Don't Toil

1 cup	soft bread crumbs	250 mL
1	medium onion, finely chopped	1
3 tbsp.	chopped green pepper	45 mL
2	slices bacon, cut into 1/4" (1 cm) pieces	2
1/4 cup	melted butter or bacon drippings	60 mL
24	cherrystone clams on the half shell	24

Combine all ingredients, except clams, in a bowl, mixing thoroughly. Cover each clam with the crumb mixture, gently packing the topping into each shell. Place the clams on an oven sheet under the broiler for about 10 minutes, until you are satisfied the bacon has cooked. Remove from oven and serve immediately.

Serves 2.

Pro's Tip:
Cherrystone clams, like littleneck clams, are also called quahogs. Their small size appeals to the gourmet as being bite-size and very tasty. Bought fresh, they should be washed 2-3 times to rid them of sand. To open more easily, cover them with water for 5 minutes, then gently lift, inserting a sharp knife in the opening, cutting through the muscle holding the shells together.

Sandtraps:
Golfers landing in them often refer to being "on the beach" or "in the kitty litter."

16

Corey's Cold Lobster Présenté

4	cooked lobsters	4
1 bunch	baby carrots, stems removed	1 bunch
4	baking potatoes	4
1 cup	butter	250 mL
1	lemon, cut into wedges	1

Break off all lobster claws, tail and body claws. With sharp scissors, cut away the soft membrane below the main body shell. Remove lobster flesh from body cavity and wash off shell. With a combination of a sharp knife, a 2-tined fork and a shell cracker, remove the lobster meat from the tail and entire front claws. Discard the cartilage from the claws. Arrange the lobster meat on 4 separate plates with the body shell in the middle as if the lobster was still in its shell. Slice the baby carrots lengthwise; place in a pot of water, and bring to a boil. Cook until carrots are softened but not mushy. Wash the potatoes; pierce with a fork; grease lightly with butter and place in microwave on high for 10-12 minutes. When potatoes and carrots are ready, melt the butter. Pour a 5" (13 cm) round pool in the middle of each plate, after lifting away the body shell. Place a baked potato in each shell and return to plate on top of the butter. Carefully lay the carrot spears to each side of the shell to give the appearance of claws. Garnish with lemon wedges.

Serves 4.

Pro's Tip:
This recipe takes time and precision, but its presentation will bring raves from your guests. Savor their praise!

17

Shelley's Seafloor and Garden Colorbration

2 tbsp.	dry white wine	30 mL
1 tbsp.	cornstarch	15 mL
2 tsp.	soy sauce	10 mL
1 lb.	sea scallops, sliced	500 g
2 tbsp.	olive oil	30 mL
2	garlic cloves, minced	2
1	medium red onion, diced	1
1 cup	broccoli florets	250 mL
1 cup	diced carrots	250 mL
1/4 cup	water	60 mL

Combine the white wine, cornstarch and soy sauce. Pour the mixture over the scallops and let stand for 20 minutes. Add olive oil and garlic to a hot wok. Next, add the onions, broccoli and carrots. Stir-fry the mixture over high heat for 30 seconds. Add the scallop mixture and continue to stir-fry for an additional 2 minutes. Reduce the heat to medium, add water, cover and cook for a further 2 minutes. Serve immediately, with rice.

Serves 4.

Pro's Tip:
This is an excellent recipe for experimentation. Try different types of vegetables, like snow peas, bean sprouts, etc. Keep the total quantity of vegetables to approximately 2 cups (500 mL). Salting the vegetables will draw out more flavor.

Murphy's law of golf:
If two balls are in the sandtrap, yours is in the footprint.

3. Greens
(Salads)

Whether it be as monstrous as the fifth green at the International Golf Club in Bolton, Mass., with an area that is just shy of 30,000 square feet, or the postage stamp-sized green at a local par three course, this beautiful plot of contoured green grass can be your most formidable enemy or your best friend. The strokes on this surface account for nearly half your total score. Similarly, the size and choice of salad relates directly to your choice for the main course.

Hale's Caesar Salad

2	medium or large heads romaine lettuce	2
1	loaf unsliced bread (French, white, or pumpernickel)	1
1 1/4 cups	olive oil	300 mL
3 tbsp.	minced garlic	45 mL
1 tsp.	garlic powder	5 mL
1/2 tsp.	celery salt	2 mL
1/2 tsp.	onion powder	2 mL
10	anchovy fillets	10
10	capers	10
1 tsp.	finely grated lemon rind	5 mL
1 tsp.	coarsely ground black pepper	5 mL
1 tbsp.	Worcestershire sauce	15 mL
1 tbsp.	fresh lemon juice	15 mL
2 dashes	cayenne pepper	2 dashes
1/2 cup	grated Parmesan cheese	125 mL
2	eggs	2

The Lettuce: Tear the romaine leaves into pieces, wash and spin dry. Place leaves in a cloth towel and refrigerate to chill.

The Croûtons: Dice 1/2 of bread into 3/4" (2 cm) cubes. Cover bottom of large frying pan with 1/2 cup (125 mL) olive oil. When oil is medium hot, sauté 1 tbsp. (15 mL) of minced garlic for 30 seconds, stirring well. On medium heat, add all bread cubes, stirring constantly until all bread is coated with oil. As bread is browning, sprinkle with garlic powder, celery salt and onion powder, adding slightly more oil if necessary. When croûtons appear toasted, place them on a paper towel and set aside to cool. If croûtons are too oily, toast briefly in the oven.

Continued on next page

20

• •

The Dressing: In a large wooden salad bowl, mash the anchovies and capers into a paste using a fork; add a dash of oil. Add remaining minced garlic, lemon rind, ground black pepper, Worcestershire sauce, lemon juice and cayenne pepper. Remove dressing to a small bowl.

The Salad: Toss all Romaine in salad bowl. Add 1/2 cup (125 mL) of olive oil, while tossing, to coat every leaf. Return the reserved dressing to the salad, spreading it as evenly as possible throughout. Add the Parmesan cheese, tossing again. Break eggs in the bowl which held the reserved dressing; stir briefly, then pour over the salad and toss again. Add the croûtons and give one final toss. Serve the salad immediately, with slices of the remaining bread and a hearty wine of your choice.

Serves 6-8.

Pro's Tip:
This is the only 600-yard hole on the course. It may seem extremely long, but it is easily reachable in regulation. It takes at least 1 hour to make, and should be made in the same room as your guests or you'll miss the start of the dinner party. If you can't spare the time at the last minute, prepare the lettuce and croûtons ahead.

Definition of net score:
The score you will admit to the next day.

21

Sally's Salad, with Spinach and Spice

1 pkg.	fresh spinach	1 pkg.
3/4 cup	olive oil	175 mL
1/4 cup	vinegar	60 mL
1 tsp.	salt	5 mL
1-3	garlic cloves, minced	1-3
dash	Worcestershire sauce	dash
3 tbsp.	creamed cottage cheese	45 mL
1/3 cup	grated Parmesan cheese	75 mL
1	medium white onion, sliced into rings	1
1/2 lb.	fresh large mushrooms, sliced vertically	250 g
10	strips bacon, cooked crisp	10

Wash and drain spinach; remove stems and place in a large salad bowl. In a blender, combine olive oil, vinegar, salt, garlic and Worcestershire sauce; blend for 20 seconds. Add cottage cheese and blend at medium speed for a further 20 seconds. Refrigerate dressing until chilled. Add Parmesan cheese to spinach and toss. Add onion rings, mushrooms and crisp bacon broken into bits; toss again. Shake dressing and pour over salad just prior to serving.

Serves 4-6.

Recipe pictured opposite page 80.

Pro's Tip:
1 clove of garlic for the weak and 3 cloves for the hearty. This is a terrific summer party salad that will leave your guests begging for the recipe.

Carol's Carrotomato
Side Salad

2	large tomatoes	2
	whole lettuce leaves	
4	carrots	4
	green onions, chopped	
	pepper, to taste	
	oil and vinegar dressing	

Cut 1/2" (1.3 cm) slices of tomatoes and place 1 on each lettuce leaf. Finely shred the carrots and toss with the chopped green onions. Mound the carrots over the tomato slices. Sprinkle with pepper and serve with an oil and vinegar dressing.

Serves 4.

Pro's Tip:
This exceptionally colorful salad is a popular summer luncheon treat and can be garnished with cucumber slices and olives to extend the effect.

Dance Floor:
The green. Commonly referred to by golfers who are not proud of their chip shot, but at least it landed on some part of the green. However far it may be from the pin, the golfer is allowed a chance to putt and relates "At least I'm on the dance floor."

23

Andy's Anchovy Antipasti

1	bunch celery	1
1/3 cup	olive oil	75 mL
2 x 2 oz.	tins anchovy fillets in oil	2 x 50 g
3	garlic cloves, chopped	3
	freshly ground pepper, to taste	

Cut all celery stalks into 2" (5 cm) lengths and cut several 1 1/2" (4 cm) cuts from the same end of each piece. Place celery in a bowl of cold water and refrigerate at least 3 hours, or until the cut ends have fanned out. In a blender, combine olive oil, anchovies in their oil and garlic. Blend for 2 minutes until smooth. Dry celery; place in a serving bowl. Toss with dressing until each piece of celery is lightly coated. Grind fresh pepper over celery, serve immediately.

Serves 6.

Recipe pictured opposite page 16.

Pro's Tip:
For added flair, surround the antipasti with cherry tomatoes and artichoke hearts.

Food for thought:
Jack Nicklaus has dominated the Masters Golf Tournament like no other golfer in history. His record 6 victories came in 1963, 1965, 1966, 1972, 1975 and 1986. He has also finished second on 4 occasions.

4. Hooks
(Fish)

A hook is a ball which, seemingly of its own volition, chooses to make a sharp left turn and leave the route that has been planned. It is also a piece of fishing gear with which you can catch some of the following tasty morsels. After some rounds of golf, you may wish you had stuck to the fishing type of hooks.

Barb's Bacon-Wrapped
Fish Fillets

1/4 cup	butter	60 mL
1 tbsp.	parsley flakes	15 mL
8	slices bacon	8
4	red snapper fillets	4
	salt and pepper, to taste	
1	lemon, sliced	1

In a small saucepan, melt the butter and stir in parsley flakes. Place bacon strips between paper towels on a microwave-safe plate and microwave on high for 3 minutes to partially cook and drain away some fat. Wrap 2 bacon strips around each fish fillet. Place wrapped fillets on a 12 x 12" (30 x 30 cm) sheet of aluminum foil. Sprinkle salt and pepper over fillets, to taste. Place lemon slices on fillets and drizzle parsley butter over them. Completely seal the fillets in the aluminum foil; place packages flat on a barbecue grill, over medium heat. Turn after 5 minutes and cook a further 7 minutes. Open the package and test the fish with a fork. When it separates into flakes, it's time to enjoy.

Serves 4.

Pro's Tip:
Various types of fillets could be used with this recipe. However, with red snapper, it provides not only excellent flavor and value, its eye-catching color presents well. To further accent the color, lightly sprinkle paprika over the fillets.

26

Greg's Gold Medal
Garlic-Fried Breaded Shrimp

2 cups	cooked long-grain white rice	500 mL
8	romaine leaves	8
1 cup	dry bread or cracker crumbs	250 mL
1/2 cup	all-purpose flour	125 mL
2	garlic cloves, minced	2
2 tbsp.	butter	30 mL
1 1/2 lbs.	fresh shrimp, medium to large, shells removed	750 g
1 cup	milk	250 mL
1	egg, beaten	1
	paprika	
	garlic powder (optional)	
12	cherry tomatoes	12
8	lemon wedges	8

Prepare the white rice and keep warm. Place 2 large romaine lettuce leaves on each of 4 plates. Mix together the crumbs and flour in a bag or a container which can be sealed. In a separate dish, mix together the milk and egg. In a large frying pan over medium heat, melt butter and sauté the minced garlic approximately 30 seconds. Dip the fresh shrimp, several at a time, in the milk mixture, then coat with the flour and crumbs by shaking in the bag or container. Place all the shrimp in the frying pan together, turning quickly to coat all shrimp with the garlic butter. Fry on medium heat for 3-5 minutes, until shrimp are cooked, being careful not to overcook. Sprinkle with paprika, for coloring, and extra garlic powder if desired. Divide cooked rice over the romaine leaves, and place shrimp within rice bed. Garnish with cherry tomatoes and lemon wedges. Serve immediately.

Serves 4.

Recipe pictured opposite page 80.

27

Chen's Fish Steaks, Oriental Style

2/3 cup	water	175 mL
1/2 cup	soy sauce	125 mL
3 tbsp.	dry white wine	45 mL
1 tsp.	granulated sugar	15 mL
2	garlic cloves, minced	2
1/2 tsp.	dried ground ginger	2 mL
4	halibut steaks	4
1/4 cup	minced green onion	60 mL

In a small saucepan, bring water, soy sauce, white wine, sugar, garlic and ginger to a boil. Reduce heat and simmer for 5 minutes. Take 4, 12" (30 cm) squares of foil. Place a fish fillet on each. Spoon sauce mixture over fish and sprinkle with green onion. Fold foil and seal securely. Arrange packets on a baking sheet. Bake 8 minutes at 350°F (180°C).

Pro's Tip:
Make sure you prefold the foil to keep the sauce mixture from running all over the counter (very messy).

Fat and thin shots:
These are improperly hit shots. The fat shot occurs when the club takes too much turf behind the ball, and the thin shot catches the ball above the center of the club head.

28

Mike's Microwaved Salmon
in White Wine Sauce

1/2 cup	dry white wine	125 mL
4 tbsp.	butter	60 mL
2 tsp.	Dijon mustard	10 mL
1 tsp.	tarragon	5 mL
pinch	white pepper	pinch
4 x 6 oz.	salmon steaks	4 x 170 g
	chopped fresh parsley	

Combine the wine, butter, mustard, tarragon and white pepper in a microwave-safe dish that is large enough to hold the fish steaks. Microwave the wine mixture on high for 1 minute. Whisk until well blended. Dip the salmon in the mixture until it is evenly coated. Arrange the fish in the sauce dish, placing the thickest parts to the outside. Cover with plastic wrap and microwave on high for about 9 minutes. Let stand for 2 minutes. Spoon remaining wine sauce over the fish, sprinkle very lightly with chopped parsley, then serve.

Serves 4.

Pro's Tip:
In today's hustle and bustle world, microwave cooking has become a method for preparing fancy, tasty meals in a very short period of time. This recipe can easily be adapted to a barbecue, placing the salmon steaks on a medium heat grill and brushing liberally with the sauce during cooking.

29

Fred's Fabulous Fish Fillets,
Italian-Style

1 tbsp.	olive oil	15 mL
1	small onion, diced	1
1/4 cup	diced green pepper	60 mL
1 tbsp.	minced parsley	15 mL
1/4 cup	chopped tomato	60 mL
1/4 cup	chopped fresh mushrooms	60 mL
1/4 tsp.	garlic powder	1 mL
	salt and pepper, to taste	
8 x 6 oz.	fish fillets, partially thawed	8 x 170 g
1 tbsp.	butter	15 mL
2 tbsp.	lemon juice	30 mL

Heat oil and sauté onion until limp. Combine onion, green pepper, parsley, tomato, mushroom and spices. Arrange half of fillets in an oiled 12" (30 cm) square baking dish. Spoon vegetables over fillets. Cover with remaining fillets. Top with butter and lemon juice. Bake at 400°F (200°C) for 15-20 minutes. Using a fork, test the fish to see if it's cooked; when it separates into flakes, it's ready for the serving plate.

Serves 6.

Pro's Tip:
Try various types of fillets until you find the fish you most enjoy in this recipe. Sole, ocean perch and orange roughy are great, but try the less expensive fish as well, keeping in mind the flavor will develop from the Italian-style filling, as well as from the fish.

5. Slices
(Meats)

One of the best definitions of mixed feelings is hearing that you have driven the ball 300 yards, only to find that 150 of them are to the right of the fairway. The effects of a slice can be overcome by hitting an exceptional second shot. However, there is no such recourse for overcooked meat.

Peter's Pocket Pepper Steak

1 tbsp.	olive oil	15 mL
1	small green pepper, cut into strips	1
1	small onion, diced	1
5	slices bacon	5
3 lbs.	round steak, in 1 piece, 2" (5 cm) thick	1.5 kg
1/2 cup	stewed tomatoes	125 mL
1/4 cup	brown sugar	60 mL
1/4 cup	red wine vinegar	60 mL
1/4 cup	dry red wine	60 mL
1	garlic clove, minced	1
1 tsp.	salt	5 mL
1	bay leaf	1
	freshly ground pepper, to taste	
1/4 cup	all-purpose flour	60 mL

Heat oil in skillet over high heat. Add green pepper and onions and stir-fry for 1 minute, or until vegetables are tender. Drain and remove from skillet; set aside. In the same skillet, cook the bacon until it is nearly done. Drain bacon, chop and set aside with vegetables. Keep the drippings in the skillet. Take a sharp knife and make a horizontal slice in the beef, creating a pocket. Stuff with the green peppers, onion and bacon pieces. Return the stuffed steak to the skillet and brown both sides. After browning, transfer the beef to a large baking dish. In the skillet, combine the tomatoes, sugar, vinegar, wine, garlic, salt and bay leaf. Season with freshly ground pepper to taste. Heat the tomato mixture until all of the sugar has dissolved. Pour 1/2 of the mixture over the beef, reserving the other 1/2 for later. Cook the meat in a 350°F (180°C) oven for 1 hour, or until the meat is tender. Check meat occasionally and spoon the juices over the beef as required to keep it moist. Remove the meat from the baking pan and place on

Continued on next page

a serving platter. Pour off and save the remaining juices; skim off the fat. Add water to the pan juices to make 2 1/2 cups (625 mL) of liquid. Stir the flour into the reserved tomato mixture until it is well blended. In a medium saucepan, combine the sauce and juices. Heat until the gravy is hot and thickened. To serve, slice the beef and pour some gravy mixture over the top.

Serves 4-6.

Buddy's Butterfly Leg of Lamb

6 lb.	leg of lamb, boned and butterflied	2.5 kg
8	garlic cloves, slivered	8
1/4 cup	olive oil	60 mL
2 tsp.	dried rosemary	10 mL
	pepper, to taste	

Make tiny slits in the lamb; insert garlic slivers into meat. Combine olive oil and rosemary; brush liberally over the meat. Apply pepper generously, as taste dictates. Barbecue over medium heat until cooked to desired level (consider using a meat thermometer).

Serves 10.

Pro's Tip:
There are 2 secrets to this recipe. First, find yourself a good butcher to properly butterfly the leg of lamb or, to butterfly a leg of lamb yourself, remove the bone carefully and cut the meat down the centre, lengthwise. Cut almost but not completely through. Open the 2 halves flat to form a butterfly shape. Second, for best results, don't overcook your lamb! Medium-cooked lamb has an internal temperature of 160°F (75°C).

33

Simon's Simple Simmered Roast Beef

3-5 lbs.	roast of beef	1.5-2.2 kg
2	medium onions, chopped	2
2	garlic cloves, chopped	2
1/2 cup	water	125 mL
1/2 cup	wine vinegar	125 mL
1 cup	dry red wine	250 mL
2 tbsp.	soy sauce	30 mL
2 tbsp.	Worcestershire sauce	30 mL
1 tsp.	dried rosemary	5 mL
1/2 tsp.	dry mustard	2 mL
	freshly ground pepper, to taste	

Place the roast, onions and garlic in a roasting pan. Prepare marinade by mixing remaining ingredients (except pepper) in a bowl. Pour marinade over the roast. Grind pepper over the roast. Cover the roasting pan and bake for 35 minutes per pound at 350°F (180°C). Add liquid during cooking as required.

Pro's Tip:
If you are using a cheaper cut of beef (shoulder, chuck, etc.), reduce the heat slightly and cook for a longer time. These types of roasts are better if cooked well-done. Sirloin or rump roasts should be cooked a shorter period of time and should be slightly on the rare side.

Food for thought:
The best cure for a horrible slice is a sharp dogleg to the right.

Tina's Tempting Pork Loin Rolls

1 cup	coarsely ground fresh pork	250 mL
	salt and pepper, to taste	
1/4 tsp.	red pepper flakes	2 mL
	garlic salt, to taste	
8 x 2 oz.	boneless pork loin chops	8 x 55 g
2 tbsp.	powdered sage	30 mL
2 cups	spinach, washed	500 mL
3 tbsp.	butter	45 mL
1	onion, finely chopped	1
1 cup	sliced fresh mushrooms	250 mL
1 cup	dry white wine	250 mL
1 cup	heavy cream (35% butterfat)	250 mL
2 tbsp.	chopped parsley	30 mL

In a mixing bowl, combine the ground pork, 1/2 tsp. (2 mL) salt, 1/4 tsp. (1 mL) pepper, red pepper flakes and garlic salt, to taste; mix thoroughly and set aside. Season the pork chops with salt and pepper. Rub with powdered sage. Pound the meat with a mallet until flattened. Next, immerse the spinach in boiling water and blanch for 1 minute. To cool, use cold water, then squeeze dry. In a saucepan, melt 2 tbsp. (30 mL) of butter and add chopped onion. Sauté the onion until limp. Add the spinach and continue cooking for an additional 3 minutes. Season the vegetables with salt and pepper. Spread the spinach mixture evenly over the flattened chops. Spread the ground pork mixture on top of the spinach. Roll up the pork chops and fasten with toothpicks. Season with salt and pepper. Melt remaining butter in a large skillet. Add the pork rolls and sauté on all sides. Add the sliced mushrooms and cook for 2 minutes. Add the wine and cream; cover and cook for 20 minutes over medium heat. Transfer the pork rolls to a serving dish and remove toothpicks. Keep rolls warm. Bring remaining sauce to a boil and continue cooking until it thickens. Season with additional salt and pepper to taste. Stir in chopped parsley. To serve, slice the rolls into pieces in order to display layers. Either spoon sauce over the rolls or present in a gravy dish.

Serves 4.

Holly's Holiday-Glazed Ham

6 lb.	fully cooked ham	2.5 kg
	whole cloves	
1-2	oranges, sliced	1-2
1/2 cup	orange marmalade	125 mL
1 tbsp.	soy sauce	15 mL
1 tsp.	prepared hot mustard	5 mL

In a shallow roasting pan, roast ham, uncovered, at 325°F (160°C) for approximately 12 minutes per pound, or until the internal temperature of the meat is 140°F (60°C). This can best be judged by using a meat thermometer that has been placed in the thickest part of the ham, away from fat and bone. About 1/2 hour before the ham is fully cooked, remove from the oven and cut the ham fat in a criss-cross pattern, making large diamond shapes on the meat. Place whole cloves into the diamond shapes. For dramatic effect, use cloves to attach orange slices to the outside of the ham. Prepare the glaze by combining the marmalade, soy sauce and hot mustard in a small saucepan; heat until the mixture is completely melted. Brush the mixture liberally over the ham. Return the ham to the oven; increase the temperature to 375°F (190°C), and cook for an additional 1/2 hour. Routinely brush the ham with more glaze mixture during this final cooking period. Remove the ham from the oven, slice, and serve immediately.

Serves 10.

Pro's Tip:
To impress the in-laws, complete your holiday entrée with Betsy's Beautiful Broccoli Bake (page 59) and Pierre's Potatoes au Gratin (page 60). To really impress them, try not to mention how you'd rather be on the golf course than cooking the main course.

6. Birdies

(Poultry)

A birdie is one of the reasons for living. No matter how bad your round may have been, one birdie makes you come back. While a birdie is one stroke under par, the following birdie recipes are way above par.

Debbie's Mustard and Marmalade Chicken

1/3 cup	Dijon mustard	75 mL
1 tbsp.	orange marmalade	15 mL
6	boneless chicken breasts	6
1/2 cup	chicken stock	125 mL
3/4 cup	whipping cream	175 mL
	salt and pepper, to taste	
	orange slices	
	chopped parsley	

Mix mustard and marmalade. Place chicken is a small, lightly greased roasting pan. Brush with half the mustard mixture. Bake in 375°F (190°C) oven for 20 minutes. Turn chicken over and baste with remaining sauce. Bake 10 minutes longer. Remove chicken and cover with foil to keep warm. Skim fat from roasting pan. Add chicken stock and boil for 5 minutes. Pour liquid into a small saucepan. Add cream and, whisking constantly, boil until sauce has thickened. Season with salt and pepper. Ladle sauce over chicken and garnish with orange slices and parsley.

Serves 6.

Pro's Tip:
Substitute white wine for the chicken stock. Complete the adventure by serving with white or wild rice to soak up the excess sauce. Boneless chicken breasts that have been individually quick frozen (IQF) provide a more tender meat but tend to shrink more than fresh chicken breasts. Do not thaw IQF breasts before placing in the oven, but they will need to be cooked an extra 15 minutes.

Rob's Remarkable
Chicken Corden Bleu

2 tbsp.	butter	30 mL
2	green onions, finely chopped	2
3 tbsp.	flour	45 mL
1 1/2 cups	chicken stock	375 mL
1/4 cup	dry white wine	60 mL
	thyme	
2 tbsp.	table cream	30 mL
4	boneless, skinless, fresh chicken	4
	breasts pounded 1/4" (1 cm) thick	
4	slices Black Forest-style ham	4
2	slices Swiss cheese, halved	2
	flour, seasoned with salt and	
	pepper, to taste	
	butter	

In a skillet, melt the butter and gently cook the onions. Blend in flour and cook for 1 minute. Gradually add the chicken stock, wine, a pinch of thyme and cream. Cook gently until thickened. Top each chicken breast with ham and cheese. Roll up and secure with toothpicks. Dredge in the seasoned flour, let stand for a few minutes, then dredge again. Sauté briefly in butter with seam side down first, to seal the edges. Place chicken rolls in a 9" (23 cm) casserole with seam side down, cover with sauce. Bake, covered, for 30 minutes at 350°F (180°C).

Serves 2-4.

Pro's Tip:
For a quick alternative to the above recipe, dip the prepared filled chicken breasts in melted butter, then roll in seasoned bread crumbs. Place on a microwave-safe dish and cook on high for 10 minutes. Let stand for 5 minutes before serving.

39

Fran's Fruit-Glazed
Cornish Hens

2	Cornish hens	2
12 oz.	can prunes, drained	341 mL
6 oz.	frozen concentrated orange juice	175 mL
1 cup	coarse bread crumbs	250 mL
1/2 cup	canned cranberry sauce	125 mL
1 tsp.	sage	5 mL
1	orange, sliced	1

Cut Cornish hens in half lengthwise to serve 4 people. In a blender, purée the prunes and orange juice for a delicious glaze. Combine the bread crumbs, cranberries and sage for the stuffing. Place the orange slices on the bottom of a lightly greased 10 x 16" (30 x 40 cm) oven pan. Form stuffing into 4 equal portions and place on the orange slices. Position the 4 Cornish Hen halves over the stuffing, skin side up. Bake for 2 hours in a preheated oven at 325°F (160°C). After the first 60 minutes, baste the hens with the glaze. Baste again every 15 minutes until cooked, making sure that the juices in the hens run clear when the meat is pierced with a fork. Serve on a large platter. Do not disturb the formation of hen over orange slices, capturing the stuffing. Top with remaining glaze for final presentation.

Serves 4.

Pro's Tip:
This main course is well-suited to be served over, or accompanied by, wild rice and Brussels sprouts for a late autumn delight. These may be the best birdies you've had all year.

40

Georgia's Peachy
Spiced Chicken

1 tbsp.	oil	15 mL
4	fresh boneless, skinless chicken breasts	4
1 cup	barbecue sauce	250 mL
14 oz.	can sliced peaches	398 mL

Heat oil in a frying pan and fry chicken 3 minutes. Combine barbecue sauce with peach syrup and pour over chicken. Cover frying pan and simmer for 30 minutes, turning occasionally. Add peach slices during last 15 minutes of cooking. Serve hot.

Serves 4.

Pro's Tip:
For general family eating, use a mild barbecue sauce. For real nice 'n' spicy, add some hot sauce to the mixture.

Food for thought:
In 1987 and 1988, Dan Forsman had 2 years of shot making that can be summed up best as "birdie, birdie, birdie." For both years he led the men's tour in number of birdies made with 409 and 465 respectively.

41

Lee's Salsafied Turkey Cutlets

1/4 cup	all-purpose flour	60 mL
1	garlic clove, minced	1
1/4 tsp.	paprika	1 mL
1/4 tsp.	freshly ground pepper	1 mL
1/4 tsp.	chili powder	1 mL
4	turkey cutlets (boneless turkey breast cut into 1/2" (1.3 cm) thick cutlets)	4
2 tbsp.	olive oil	30 mL
1/4 cup	medium or hot salsa	60 mL
1/2 cup	shredded brick cheese	125 mL

Combine flour, garlic, paprika, pepper and chili powder in a bag or sealable plastic container. Place cutlets in the container, seal, and shake lightly until the cutlets are completely covered with the flour mixture. In a large skillet, heat the oil. Cook the cutlets over medium-high heat for 3-4 minutes on each side, or until lightly browned with no pink inside. Reduce the heat. Spoon 1 tbsp. (15 mL) of salsa onto the center of each cutlet. Sprinkle the cheese evenly over the cutlets. Cover and cook for an additional 5 minutes, or until cheese has melted. Serve with additional salsa.

Serves 4.

Pro's Tip:
Turn this into a Mexican fiesta with refried beans, hot rice and nacho chips with guacamole dip. Guaranteed to leave you both salsafied and satisfied.

7. The Mulligan
(Stews)

Some refer to this as the second shot that no one saw you take. In reality, during a friendly game this illegal second shot is permitted, usually on the first hole when no other foursomes are watching or waiting. Perhaps the toughest moral issue for a golfer to face is how to score a hole in one that has been achieved on a mulligan. Stews also allow the chef to rethink any mistakes and add just about anything to round out a full pot.

Greg's Gumbo with Gusto

8	chicken drumsticks	8
2 quarts	water	2 L
1/4 cup	vegetable oil	60 mL
1/4 cup	all-purpose flour	60 mL
1 lb.	okra, in 1/2" (1.3 cm) pieces	500 g
1 cup	chopped onion	250 mL
1/2 cup	chopped celery	125 mL
2	garlic cloves, minced	2
14 oz.	can tomatoes	398 mL
1/2 tsp.	thyme	2 mL
1	bay leaf	1
1 tsp.	salt	5 mL
1 tsp.	red pepper flakes	5 mL
1 lb.	peeled and deveined raw shrimp	500 g
1/2 lb.	smoked sausage, in 1/2" (1.3 cm) chunks	250 mL
1/4 cup	chopped parsley	60 mL

In a large pot, bring the water to a boil; drop in chicken drumsticks and cook for 15 minutes. Remove the chicken; allow water to stand, discarding the fat skimmed off the top. Heat oil in a heavy skillet over low heat. Stir in flour and brown slowly, stirring constantly, to assure flour has not stuck to bottom. Set aside the roux when dark brown. In a heavy soup pot, heat oil and sauté the okra, onions and celery until turning brown. Add minced garlic and sauté 1 extra minute. Stir in reserved water, roux, tomatoes, thyme, bay leaf, salt and pepper flakes. After bringing to a boil, cover and simmer for 45 minutes. Remove and discard the bay leaf. Add shrimp, sausage, and chicken. Cover and simmer a further 15 minutes. Stir in parsley. Serve over a mound of cooked white rice, about 1/2 cup (125 mL) per serving, in large, wide, soup bowls.

Serves 8.

44

John's Hot Beef Chili

2 lbs.	blade steak or roast, cubed	1 kg
2 x 12 oz.	bottles beer	2 x 341 mL
3 tbsp.	soy sauce	45 mL
1 tbsp.	Worcestershire sauce	15 mL
2 tbsp.	vegetable oil	30 mL
1	onion, chopped	1
3	garlic cloves, crushed	3
1	green bell pepper, chopped	1
1	red bell pepper, chopped	1
1-3	jalapeño peppers, finely chopped	1-3
28 oz.	can red kidney beans	796 mL
10 oz.	can beef broth	284 mL
14 oz.	can brown beans	398 mL
28 oz.	can plum tomatoes	796 mL
1/2 cup	dry red wine	125 mL
2 tbsp.	chili powder	30 mL
2 tsp.	cumin	10 mL
	salt and pepper, to taste	

To prepare the beef, cube and place in a bowl, adding the beer, soy sauce and Worcestershire sauce. Refrigerate for up to 24 hours. Remove beef and discard marinade. Heat oil in a skillet; add beef and brown 5-8 minutes, stirring occasionally. Add onion, garlic, bell peppers and jalapeño peppers. Cook for 3 minutes, or until the vegetables are tender-crisp. Stir frequently. In a slow cooker, combine the beef and vegetable mixture and the remaining ingredients. Cook on the high setting for 1 hour, then reduce to low setting and cook for another 2-3 hours. If you don't have a slow cooker, simmer gently in a large heavy saucepan, covered, for about 3 hours. Serve with a hearty red wine, crusty loaf of bread and a chef's salad.

Serves 8.

45

Pablo's Picante Chili

1 tbsp.	olive oil	15 mL
1 lb.	pork tenderloin, cubed	500 g
1	onion, chopped	1
2	garlic cloves, minced	2
4 cups	salsa	1 L
14 oz.	can whole tomatoes, not drained, cut up	398 mL
28 oz.	can red kidney beans	796 mL
1/2 cup	shredded lettuce	125 mL
1 cup	sour cream	250 mL
1 cup	diced tomatoes	250 mL
4 oz.	can green chilies, chopped	114 mL
1 cup	coarsely grated Cheddar cheese	250 mL

Heat the oil in a large saucepan over medium-high heat. Add the pork and onions. Cook until the pork is cooked through (no longer pink). Add garlic, salsa, tomatoes and kidney beans. Cover and reduce the heat to medium. Continue cooking until beans and meat are tender, about 1 hour, stirring occasionally. To serve, ladle the chili mixture into a bowl, then top with shredded lettuce, sour cream, diced tomatoes, green chilies and cheese, according to individual taste.

Serves 4.

Pro's Tip:
This chili will be as hot as you want, depending on the type of salsa that you choose. For added heat, try some finely chopped jalapeño peppers or Louisiana hot sauce.

Pierre's Old-Country Stew

1 lb.	lamb shoulder roast	500 g
1 lb.	pork butt roast	500 g
1 lb.	beef chuck roast	500 g
1	large onion, coarsely chopped	1
2	garlic cloves, crushed	2
1	bunch parsley	1
	dry white wine	
4	large potatoes	4
2	carrots	2
1	large onion, diced	1
1	bay leaf	1
	salt and pepper, to taste	
2 tbsp.	chopped parsley	30 mL

Cut the 3 varieties of meat into 1" (2.5 cm) chunks. Place in a shallow dish. Add coarsely chopped onion and a garlic clove. Tie the bunch of parsley wth string and add to the dish. Add white wine until most of the meat is covered. Cover and refrigerate overnight. Peel and coarsely slice the potatoes and carrots. Rinse the vegetables under lukewarm water. Evenly spead 1/2 of the vegetables over the bottom of a large roasting pan. Remove the meats from the marinade and place on the potatoes. Add diced onions, a clove of garlic, and the bay leaf. Add remaining potatoes and carrots, then season with salt and pepper. Drain the marinade through a strainer into the stew. Add additional white wine to bring the level of liquids to almost cover all of the stew. In a preheated oven, cook the stew, covered, for 2 1/2 hours at 350°F (180°C). Sprinkle with parsley and serve immediately.

Serves 4.

47

Owen's Oxford Oxtail Stew

1 tsp.	salt	5 mL
1/2 tsp.	freshly ground pepper	2 mL
1/3 cup	all-purpose flour	75 mL
3 lbs.	oxtails, in 2" (5 cm) pieces	1.5 kg
2 tbsp.	olive oil	30 mL
5	carrots, thickly sliced	5
1	large Spanish onion, chopped	1
1 cup	chopped celery	250 mL
1 cup	sliced fresh mushrooms	250 mL
2	garlic cloves, finely sliced	2
2 1/2 cups	beef broth	625 mL
2 tbsp.	tomato paste	30 mL
1	bay leaf, broken	1
1/4 tsp.	dried thyme, crushed	1 mL

Combine the salt, pepper and flour in a container which can be sealed. Place the oxtail pieces in the container; seal and shake until oxtails are coated with the flour mixture. In a Dutch oven, heat the oil and add half of the oxtail pieces. Brown on all sides. Remove oxtails and drain. Repeat with remaining meat. Upon completion, drain off all but 2 tbsp. (30 mL) of the oil. Add the carrots, onion, celery, mushrooms and garlic and cook until the onion and celery are tender. Stir in the remaining ingredients and bring to a boil. Add the oxtails. Cover the stew and simmer for 2 hours, or until the meat is tender.

Serves 6.

Pro's Tip:
For best results, skim off excess fat from the stew before serving. As an alternative to oxtails, consider using braising beef ribs.

8. A Hot Round
(Hot 'n' Spicy)

Having a hot round adds considerably to the enjoyment of the game because it is all too infrequent. Similarly, the occasional hot dish added to your meal will add both spice and pleasure.

Beth's Black Bean Salsa
(A Little Hot!)

1/2 cup	dried black beans, soaked overnight	125 mL
3 tbsp.	olive oil	45 mL
5	ripe tomatoes, halved, drained and diced	5
1	red onion, diced	1
2 tbsp.	chopped coriander (also known as cilantro or Chinese parsley)	30 mL
3	garlic cloves, minced	3
3	jalapeño peppers, chopped	3
2 tbsp.	lime juice	30 mL
	salt and pepper, to taste	

Cook the soaked black beans in salted water until very tender, about 1-1 1/2 hours. Drain. In a large mixing bowl, combine the beans with the remaining ingredients. Let the salsa stand for 2 hours to allow the flavors to develop. Drain off any excess water before serving.

Makes about 4 cups (1 L) of salsa.

Recipe pictured opposite page 48.

Pro's Tip:
For a sensational taste treat, spread this salsa on a flour tortilla shell, then top with strips of smoked salmon, grated asiago cheese and capers. Roll tightly, then serve.

Charlie's Chunky Salsa
(Youch!! That's Hot!!)

6	serrano chilies	6
2	large ripe tomatoes	2
1	Spanish onion, chopped	1
1/4 cup	chopped English cucumber	60 mL
2 tsp.	minced coriander	10 mL
2 tbsp.	olive oil	30 mL
1/2 tsp.	salt	2 mL
1/4 cup	water	60 mL

Remove stems from chilies and tomatoes. Using a food processor, coarsely chop the tomatoes and chilies together. Add the onion, cucumber and coriander and continue processing until thoroughly chopped and mixed. Remove from food processor to a large serving bowl and add the oil, salt and water.

Makes about 4 cups (1 L) of salsa.

Recipe pictured opposite page 48.

Pro's Tip:
This salsa is best served at room temperature the same day that it is made. After handling them, be careful not to transfer the bright clean heat of the serrano chilies from your hands to your eyes, unless you want to cry as hard as you do after missing the final putt needed to win the club championship.

Screamingly Ultra Hot* Salsa

* To be used as a dipping sauce whenever
you need to shed some real tears

3	habañero (Scotch Bonnet) chilies	3
1	red onion	1
1/4 cup	freshly squeezed orange juice	60 mL
2 tbsp.	lemon juice	30 mL

Using a sharp knife, coarsely chop the chilies and onion. Remove to a bowl and add the citrus juices. Serve at room temperature within an hour.

Makes about 1 cup (250 mL) of salsa.

Pro's Tip:
The habañero chili, which is native to the Caribbean, is one of the world's hottest chilies. By one measure, it is 100 times hotter than the jalapeño pepper. The secret to this salsa is the citrus juice which draws the heat out of the pepper. The longer it sits, the hotter it becomes. Therefore, appropriate caution should be taken both in the preparation and use of this sauce. Wear rubber gloves when handling peppers and do not touch your lips or eyes.

Food for thought:
The hottest round registered in a men's professional golf tournament is 59. This incredible score has been achieved twice, by Al Geiberger in the 1977 Memphis Classic, and matched by Chip Beck in the 1991 Las Vegas Invitational.

52

Louisiana Chicken Wings

2 lbs.	chicken wings, tips removed	1 kg
1/4 cup	olive oil	60 mL
1/4 cup	melted butter	60 mL
1/4 cup	barbecue sauce	60 mL
1/2 cup	Louisiana hot sauce	125 mL

Separate the chicken wing drums from flats and place all parts in salted boiling water. Return to a boil and cook for 7 1/2 minutes. Remove wings from water and pat dry. Heat oil to 365°F (185°C) in a skillet and add chicken parts. Deep-fry wings for 2 minutes, or until outside edges are crispy. Remove from oil and place in a large bowl that can be sealed. Drizzle with melted butter. Pour barbecue and hot sauce over wings and seal container. Shake well until wings are completely coated. Serve immediately.

Serves 2.

Recipe pictured opposite page 48.

Pro's Tip:
For even hotter wings, use proportionally more hot sauce and less of the barbecue sauce. For milder wings, use more barbecue sauce and less hot sauce. This is a secret recipe from one of the finest chicken wing producers in North America. Don't tell anyone where you got it.

In a match, never burden your opponent with the sole responsibility of counting all his strokes.

53

Teri's Taco-Seasoned
Pork Tenderloin

1 1/4 oz.	envelope hot taco seasoning mix	35 g
2 tbsp.	brown sugar	30 mL
1/2 tsp.	ground cinnamon	2 mL
2 lb.	pork tenderloin	1 kg
1 cup	hot salsa	250 mL
1/4 cup	water	60 mL
1/4 cup	lime juice	60 mL
2	large garlic cloves, crushed	2

Combine taco seasonings, sugar and cinnamon. Rub half of seasoning mixture over the pork. Bake at 350°F (180°C) for 10 minutes. Combine salsa, water, lime juice, garlic and remaining seasoning mix. Pour over the pork and roast an additional 15-20 minutes. Remove pork from oven and let stand for 10 minutes. Thinly slice pork and arrange on a platter. Spoon the salsa mixture over pork. Serve with rice.

Serves 4.

Pro's Tip:
For a little added zip, use tequila instead of water.

A hot year:
In 1945, Byron Nelson set a single season record of 18 wins on the men's tour. Add to this his record of 19 consecutive rounds of golf under 70 and you would have to say he had a relatively good year.

9. Playing In The Rough
(Vegetables)

I t must be healthy to hit your ball into the rough, otherwise most golfers wouldn't spend so much time there. Likewise, adding the color of a fine vegetable dish to your dinner is equally attractive, tasty and nutritious.

Gary's Garlic Mushrooms

3 tbsp.	butter	45 mL
1	onion, chopped	1
3-4	garlic cloves, minced	3-4
1/2	green bell pepper, chopped	1/2
1/2	red bell pepper, chopped	1/2
1 lb.	fresh mushrooms, sliced	500 g
1/2 cup	dry white wine	125 mL
2 tbsp.	soy sauce	30 mL
1 tbsp.	Worcestershire sauce	15 mL
	salt and pepper, to taste	

In a large skillet, melt butter and add onions, garlic and peppers. After 2 minutes, add mushrooms and sauté for an additional 2 minutes. Add wine, soy sauce and Worcestershire sauce. Cover and cook slowly for 5-15 minutes, or until all vegetables are tender. Add salt and pepper to taste.

Serves 4.

Recipe pictured opposite page 96.

Pro's Tip:
This is a perfect side dish for a porterhouse or sirloin strip steak. It can be served by itself or over rice. Don't be suprised when mushrooms lose 2/3 of their volume as the moisture fries out.

You know you're *having a bad day when you crack open the fourth sleeve of balls.*

Stan's Outstanding Stuffed Zucchini

2	large zucchini	2
	butter	
1/2 cup	sliced fresh mushrooms	125 mL
1 cup	asparagus tips	250 mL
1	small onion, finely chopped	1
1 cup	grated medium or old Cheddar cheese	250 mL
1/2 cup	sour cream	125 mL
1/2 cup	dried bread crumbs	125 mL
2 tbsp.	dry white wine	30 mL
1 tsp.	paprika	5 mL
1 tsp.	parsley flakes	5 mL
	salt and pepper, to taste	
4	slices bacon, fried crisp and broken into bits	4

To prepare zucchini, scrub, trim, then halve. Place in a saucepan of boiling water for about 12 minutes. Drain off the water and cool the zucchini. Scoop out the seeds. Place zucchini in a well-buttered baking dish. In a skillet, melt 1 tbsp. (15 mL) butter and fry the mushrooms for 2 minutes, or until slightly browned. Remove from heat and allow to cool. In a bowl, combine the mushrooms, asparagus tips, onion, cheese, sour cream, bread crumbs and wine. Add salt and pepper to taste. Blend well by hand. Divide the mixture evenly and position in the zucchini. Sprinkle paprika, parsley flakes and bacon bits over the top. Bake for 20-25 minutes at 350°F (180°C). After removing from oven, sprinkle with additional paprika and parsley flakes, to taste.

Serves 4.

Recipe pictured opposite page 96.

57

Sammy's Super Spinach

2 tbsp.	olive oil	30 mL
2	garlic cloves, crushed	2
1	Spanish onion, chopped	1
2 lbs.	spinach	1 kg
1/4 cup	dry white wine	60 mL
2	eggs, beaten	2
1 1/2 cups	grated Parmesan cheese	375 mL
	salt and pepper, to taste	
	butter	

In a skillet, heat the oil and sauté garlic and onion until limp. Wash spinach, then tear into bite-sized pieces; add to the onion mixture. Cover and cook for 2 minutes, or until spinach has wilted. Remove from heat. In a baking dish, combine the slightly cooled spinach mixture, wine, eggs and half of the cheese. Season with salt and pepper, to taste. Sprinkle with the remaining cheese and top with a few dabs of butter. Bake at 375°F (190°C) for 15 minutes.

Serves 4.

Fresh Mushroom Sauce

2 tbsp.	butter	30 mL
8	large mushrooms, chopped	8
1/2	medium onion, finely chopped	1/2
1 tbsp.	all-purpose flour	15 mL
	salt and pepper, to taste	
1 cup	chicken broth	250 mL
3/4 cup	dry white wine	175 mL
3 tbsp.	sweet cream	45 mL
	lemon juice, to taste	

Continued on next page

58

Fresh Mushroom Sauce Continued

Heat butter and sauté mushrooms and onions for 15 minutes, or until the onions are lightly browned and the mushrooms are soft. Add flour and seasonings and continue cooking, stirring until the mixture is thoroughly blended. Take care not to brown the flour. Slowly add the broth and, when smooth, add the wine and cream. Add lemon juice to taste and simmer the sauce for 10 minutes. Serve immediately.

Makes about 3 cups (750 mL) of sauce.

Betsy's Beautiful Broccoli Bake

2 cups	cooked wild rice	500 mL
	broccoli, enough for 4 servings	
10 oz.	can cream of mushroom soup	284 mL
2 tbsp.	mayonnaise	30 mL
3 tbsp.	milk	45 mL
1	egg, beaten	1
1 cup	grated Cheddar cheese	250 mL
	pepper, to taste	
	lemon pepper, to taste	

Place cooked wild rice in the bottom of a 3-quart (3 L) casserole. Layer broccoli over rice. Mix together the remaining ingredients and pour over the broccoli. Bake at 350°F (180°C) for 1 hour.

Serves 4.

Pro's Tip:
Sliced carrots, cauliflower or onions can be added, exchanged or mixed for variations in the flavor of the dish.

Pierre's Potatoes au Gratin

1 1/2 lbs.	potatoes	750 g
	butter	
	salt and pepper, to taste	
	nutmeg, to taste	
1	large leek, cut into rings	1
1	red pepper, diced	1
7 oz.	cereal cream	190 mL
2	eggs	2
2 tbsp.	chopped parsley	30 mL
2 tsp.	margarine, melted	10 mL
2 tsp.	dried thyme	10 mL
4 oz.	Gouda or Gruyère cheese, shredded	115 g

Boil potatoes in skins until soft. Peel and slice thinly. Lightly grease a baking dish with butter; add half of the potato slices. Sprinkle with salt, pepper and nutmeg. Layer leeks over the potatoes. Cover with remaining potato slices. Sprinkle again with salt, pepper and nutmeg. Randomly drop diced red pepper over the potatoes. Beat together the cream, eggs, parsley, margarine and thyme. Add salt, pepper and nutmeg. Pour over the potatoes. Bake in a 425°F (220°C) oven for 15 minutes. Sprinkle shredded cheese over the top and return to oven for a further 10 minutes.

Serves 6.

Pro's Tip:
This is a great accompaniment to the family's Sunday night pineapple-glazed roast ham dinner.

60

10. Making The Turn
(Sandwiches)

Sandwiched between the front and back nine is a halfway house for the sale of snacks and refreshments as you make the turn. It's a shame that more courses can't offer more of the following instead of the usual fare of hot dogs and hamburgers.

Pete's Pita Pocket
with Beef and Veggies

2/3 cup	dry red wine	150 mL
3 tbsp.	olive oil	45 mL
2	garlic cloves, minced	2
1/2 tsp.	dried crushed oregano	2 mL
1/2 tsp.	salt	2 mL
	freshly ground pepper, to taste	
1 1/2 lbs.	boneless New York strip steak	750 g
2 tbsp.	butter	30 mL
2 cups	chopped lettuce	500 mL
1 cup	diced tomato	250 mL
1 cup	diced cucumber	250 mL
1 cup	grated mozzarella cheese	250 mL
1 cup	sour cream with chopped chives	250 mL
1/2 cup	sliced black olives	125 mL
6	pieces pita pocket bread	6

Combine the wine, oil, garlic, oregano, salt and pepper. Cut the steak into 1 x 2" (2.5 x 5 cm) slices and place in the marinade. Cover and refrigerate for 24 hours. Drain the beef thoroughly. In hot butter, brown the steak on all sides and cook to desired taste. Prepare the pita pockets by opening 1 end with a sharp knife. Fill each pocket with a small amount of the beef and garnish with remaining ingredients to personal taste.

Serves 6.

Pro's Tip:
This sandwich is best when the beef is hot. However, it is also a real taste treat prepared and eaten cold as a "traveler."

Hogan's Hero:
The Six-Foot Party Sandwich

1	6' (1.85 m) loaf of bread	1
	butter	
	mayonnaise	
24 slices	processed cheese, several varieties	24 slices
35 slices	cooked meat, several varieties	35 slices
2	heads lettuce, shredded	2
	mustard	
7	large ripe tomatoes, thinly sliced	7
2	large Spanish onions, cut into rings	2
1	green pepper, seeded, cut into rings	1
1	red pepper, seeded, cut into rings	1
8 oz.	jar stuffed olives, halved	250 mL
	salad dressing	
	salt and pepper, to taste	

Place the loaf of bread on a 7' (2.15 m) long wooden plank, about 6" (15 cm) wide. As it may be difficult to find a 6' (2 m) loaf of bread, you can also use 7 or 8 sticks of French bread, all the same width. Cut off the rounded ends and place end to end on the plank. Cut the loaf or loaves in half, lengthwise, horizontally, opening completely. Spread butter from end to end, then add mayonnaise as desired. Lay slices of cheese diagonally along the bread so they overlap each other and hang over the edge of the bread. Similarly, overlap the meat slices, varying the types all the way along, back and forth. If desired, spread the meat with mustard. Next, sprinkle lettuce from end to end. Add tomato slices. Top with onion rings, pepper rings and olives. If salad dressing is desired, drizzle lightly over the vegetables from end to end. Add salt and pepper to taste. Return the top(s) to the sandwich, slice and serve. To slice, use a sharp serrated knife or, better still, an electric carving knife.

Serves 18.

Recipe pictured opposite page 48.

63

Bob's Bagel Beauties,
Quick and Tasty

3	pumpernickel bagels	3
	butter	
3 tbsp.	mayonnaise or cream cheese	45 mL
6 slices	prosciutto	6 slices
6	melon balls, halved	6

Slice the bagels in half. Toast, then lightly butter. Spread with mayonnaise or cream cheese, depending on taste. Top with a slice of prosciutto and 2 halved melon balls.

Pro's Tip:
Quick and tasty sums up this recipe very nicely. It is sometimes amazing how combining just a few simple ingredients can result in such a wonderful taste experience.

Bite:
When the ball lands on the green with sufficient backspin to keep it from rolling, it is said to "bite." Commonly requested by golfers, but rarely achieved.

Reuben's Reuben

1 tsp.	butter	5 mL
1	small onion, diced	1
14 oz.	can sauerkraut, drained	398 mL
12	thin slices of Montreal smoked meat, pastrami, or corned beef	12
6	slices, rye bread, lightly buttered	6
3	slices Swiss cheese prepared mustard	3

In a small skillet, warm butter, then sauté onion until tender. Add sauerkraut and continue cooking until heated through. Avoid browning. Place the smoked meat on a microwave-safe dish. Cook on high for 35 seconds, or until hot. On a slice of bread, place a slice of Swiss cheese. Place 4 folded slices of the smoked meat on top of the cheese; top with the sauerkraut and onion mixture. On another slice of bread, spread mustard and top off the sandwich. Repeat for 2 more sandwiches.

Serves 3.

Pro's Tip:
For presentation purposes, mix and match light or dark rye with pumpernickel slices.

Playing the front 9 at even par guarantees a 30-minute rain delay with a partner who insists on spending it in the bar.

Frank's Frank Sandwich
with Beans and Relish

2	hot dog wieners, halved	2
6	slices oat bran bread, toasted	6
	butter or margarine	
4	slices tomato	4
1/2 cup	baked brown beans	125 mL
1/4 cup	zucchini relish	60 mL

In a skillet, lightly fry the halved wieners, warming through. Spread 2 toast slices with butter, then top with 2 slices of tomato and the baked beans. Spread the remaining bread slices with the relish. Add 1 relish-spread slice to the top of a bean-covered slice. Top with 2 of the half wieners. Top again with 1 relish-spread toast, with the relish facing down. Secure with toothpicks, then cut diagonally.

Serves 2 (or 1 very hungry golfer).

Food for thought:
In professional golf, which statistics really tell the story? Between 1981 and 1990, Calvin Peete had the best driving accuracy percentage of any player on the professional tour. Between 1981 and 1983, he had the highest percentage of greens shot in regulation. And in 1984 he had the best scoring average per round. Yet, even with his hitting accuracy he won no major championships, never led in any of these years in money earnings, and is not on the list of top 50 career money leaders.

66

11. Chip Shots
(Dips and Spreads)

A good chipper is like a middle reliever in baseball: unmemorable perhaps, but essential to achieve victory. Dips and spreads, with chips, crackers or breads, act in the same way: though only a small part of the overall meal, like hors d'oeuvres, they increase the chances of dining success.

Hal's Hot Creamy
Cheese with Shrimp Dip

8 oz.	cream cheese	250 g
6.5 oz.	can broken shrimp or crab meat	184 g
2 tbsp.	ketchup or chili sauce or seafood sauce	30 mL
1 tsp.	instant minced onion	5 mL
1 tsp.	prepared mustard	5 mL
1 tsp.	Worcestershire sauce	5 mL
1/4 tsp.	garlic powder	1 mL

Combine all ingredients in a 1-quart (1 L) microwave-safe casserole. Microwave on high 3-4 minutes, or until warm, stirring once, during the cooking time. Stir again, then serve with taco chips.

Serves 6.

Pro's Tip:
Along with the chips, set out some raw vegetables, such as celery, red and green pepper strips, broccoli and carrot sticks.

Chili dip:
When the swing is flubbed so badly that the turf moved goes farther than the ball.

Jose's Mexican Antipasto

Layer 1:

8 oz.	cream cheese	250 g
dash	garlic salt	dash
1/2 cup	sour cream	125 mL

Layer 2:

1	large avocado, mashed	1
1/4 tsp.	lemon juice	1 mL
1	tomato, finely chopped	1
4 oz.	green chilies, chopped	114 mL

Layer 3:

5	slices bacon, cooked crisp and diced	5
4	green onions, chopped	4
1/4 cup	chopped black olives	60 mL
1/4 cup	sliced stuffed green olives	60 mL
8 oz.	hot taco sauce	250 mL
1 cup	grated cheese	250 mL

Mix together all first layer ingredients, then spread over a 10" (25 cm) serving dish. Mix second layer ingredients together and spread over the first layer. For the third layer, sprinkle bacon, onions, black and green olives over the second layer. Then spread taco sauce over the entire surface and, finally, top with cheese. Serve cold; use taco chips to dip.

Serves 8.

Pro's Tip:
For added spiciness, add hot chilies or finely sliced jalapeño pepper to the second layer mixture.

69

Doris' "Can't Miss"
Cheese Ball

8 oz.	cream cheese	250 g
8 oz.	sharp Cheddar cheese	250 g
8 oz.	Havarti cheese	250 g
2 tbsp.	mayonnaise	30 mL
3	green onions, chopped	3
1/2	green pepper, finely chopped	1/2
1/2 cup	pimiento	125 mL
1 cup	finely chopped walnuts	250 mL

Combine all ingredients, except the walnuts, in a food processor. Shape processed mixture into a ball. Roll ball in finely chopped walnuts. Serve with your favorite chips and crackers.

Serves 10.

Pro's Tip:
Prepare the cheese ball well ahead of time (at least the previous day). The flavors seep nicely through the cheeses over a period of time. For a little more zip, consider adding some chopped hot peppers or cracked black peppercorns.

In match play, *it is important to help your opponent realize all the potential problems with his upcoming shot.*

70

Paul's Pumpernickel Bread
with Spinach Dip

1	loaf pumpernickel bread	1
1 cup	sour cream	250 mL
1 cup	mayonnaise	250 mL
10 oz.	chopped frozen spinach, thawed and drained	283 g
1 1/2 oz.	envelope onion soup mix	40 g

Cut a slice off the top of the pumpernickel loaf and hollow out the bread as a bowl for your dip. Place the hollowed loaf on a large serving dish. Cut the removed bread into cubes and place around hollowed loaf. In a large bowl, mix thoroughly all of the remaining ingredients. Pour the mixture into the hollowed bread.

Serves 10.

Recipe pictured opposite page 16.

Pro's Tip:
It always seems with this recipe that there is more dip than bread left over. A second loaf of pumpernickel or 3-grain bread cut into cubes will take care of this problem quite nicely. Try some variations. Substitute dry vegetable soup mix and 1/4 cup (60 mL) minced onion for onion soup mix. Add 1/4-1/2 cup (60-125 mL) chopped water chestnuts. Heat the dip before putting it into the hollowed bread. Or, cover the filled loaf with the top slice, to make a lid. Wrap the loaf in aluminum foil and bake at 300°F (150°C) for 1 1/2-2 hours.

Nick's Nacho Supremo

	nacho chips	
1 cup	hot chunky salsa	250 mL
1/2 cup	diced black or stuffed green olives	125 mL
1/2 cup	diced tomatoes	125 mL
2	jalapeño peppers, sliced	2
1 cup	Cheddar or Monterey Jack cheese, shredded	250 mL

Arrange nachos 2-3 chips deep on a microwave-safe dish. Spread a layer of salsa over the chips. Add olives, tomatoes, peppers and cover with a thin layer of shredded cheese. Place in microwave, on high, for 2 minutes, or until cheese has melted.

Serves 4.

Pro's Tip:
For those who like salsa, place a small bowl to the side for extra dipping. Also, buy a big bag of nacho chips, as your guests will insist on seconds.

You know you're *having a bad day when your tee shot goes directly into the hole and your actual score is 5.*

72

12. Water Hazards
(Soups)

How to make a golfer nervous: Place 100 yards of water between him and the green. Overcoming the fear of these hazards is an integral part of your game. Don't be afraid to return soup to your daily or entertaining menu.

Mushroom, Broccoli and Cheddar Cheese Soup

3 tbsp.	butter	45 mL
1	onion, chopped	1
1	garlic clove, finely chopped	1
3/4 lb.	mushrooms, sliced	365 g
1/4 cup	all-purpose flour	60 mL
3 cups	chicken stock	750 mL
2 cups	milk	500 mL
1 cup	finely chopped cooked broccoli	250 mL
1 tsp.	salt	5 mL
	pepper, to taste	
1 1/2 cups	coarsely grated Cheddar cheese	375 mL

Melt butter in a large saucepan. Add onion and garlic. Sauté over medium heat for 3 minutes. Add mushrooms and cook over high heat until lightly browned. Sprinkle the flour over mushrooms. Cook 3-5 minutes, until flour is just lightly browned. Add chicken, stock and milk, and bring to a boil. Add broccoli, salt and pepper. Reduce heat, cover and simmer for 15 minutes. Purée the soup in small batches, then return to the pot. Add the cheese. Cook gently until the cheese has just slightly melted.

Serves 6.

Pro's Tips:

Chopped fresh parsley and cheese provides a nice garnish, if desired. Puréeing the vegetables seems like a lot of work, but it is essential to take out the lumps and provide a beautiful creamy soup. If the mixture seems too thick, add 1/4 cup (60 mL) of white wine, chicken stock or milk.

Minnie's Minestrone Soup

5 cups	chicken broth	1.25 L
3	medium carrots, sliced	3
2	celery stalks, sliced	2
1	onion, chopped	1
14 oz.	can tomatoes	398 mL
3/4 cup	dry fusilli pasta	175 mL
14 oz.	can red kidney beans, drained	398 mL
19 oz.	can chickpeas, drained	540 mL
1 cup	frozen peas	250 mL
	salt and pepper, to taste	

In large saucepan, bring broth to a boil. Add carrots, celery and onion. Stir in tomatoes, breaking apart with a fork. Simmer, covered, for 15 minutes. Cook fusilli according to package directions. Add kidney beans and chickpeas to vegetable mixture and simmer for 10 minutes. Stir fusilli and peas into soup and heat through. Season to taste with salt and pepper.

Serves 10.

Pro's Tip:
Our usual suggestion, a little hot pepper added to this soup, creates an even greater taste sensation. Believe it or not, this recipe may be the most nutritious one in the whole book.

USGA definition for a water hazard:
"Any sea, lake, pond, river, ditch, surface drainage ditch, or other open water course (regardless of whether or not it contains water) and anything of a similar nature."

75

Jocelynn's French Onion Soup

4	large onions, sliced	4
3 tbsp.	butter	45 mL
6 cups	beef broth	1.5 L
1 tsp.	salt	5 mL
1/4 tsp.	pepper	1 mL
1 tsp.	Worcestershire sauce	5 mL
6	slices French bread, toasted	6
1/2 cup	grated Parmesan cheese	125 mL
1/3 cup	shredded Swiss, Cheddar, or mozzarella cheese	75 mL

Sauté onion in butter until brown, about 15 minutes. Stir in beef broth, salt and pepper. Add Worcestershire sauce. Bring to a boil, then simmer for 30 minutes. Ladle soup into 6 oven-safe soup bowls. Place bread on top and sprinkle with cheese. Heat at 425°F (220°C) for 10 minutes, then place under broiler until the top is bubbly and lightly browned.

Serves 6.

Pro's Tip:
Sometimes with soup it is just as important when to have it as how it is made. This soup, piping hot, is great when you're coming in off an October round. Also, special onion soup bowls are a great investment if you enjoy this type of soup. Add a hearty wine and a loaf of crusty bread, then enjoy with a foursome of close friends.

Nancy's New England
Clam Chowder

1/4 lb.	bacon, cut up	115 g
1	medium onion, chopped	1
2 x 5 oz.	cans minced clams, drained, liquid reserved	2 x 142 g
2 cups	diced potatoes	500 mL
2 cups	milk	500 mL
	pepper to taste	

Cook and stir bacon and onion in 2-quart (2 L) saucepan until bacon is crisp. Add enough water to clam liquid to measure 1 cup (250 mL). Stir clam liquid, potatoes and pepper into the mixture. Heat to boiling, then reduce heat. Cover and cook, stirring in the clams after 10 minutes. Continue cooking until the potatoes are tender, about 10 minutes. Stir in milk. Heat, stirring occasionally, just until hot (do not boil).

Serves 4.

Pro's Tip:
A little hot pepper in this recipe warms up the soup quite nicely. A little dry vermouth has also been known to add a fresh flavor.

Definition of an optimist:
A golfer who has never hit the ball over 200 yards, sees a water hazard at 190 yards and says "I'm going for it!"

Hearty Chicken Soup

5 cups	chicken broth	1.25 L
3	carrots, sliced	3
2 cups	broccoli florets	500 mL
1 cup	sliced fresh mushrooms	250 mL
1 cup	sliced celery	250 mL
1	onion, chopped	1
3	garlic cloves, minced	3
1/2 cup	dry rotini	125 mL
2 cups	cubed cooked chicken	500 mL

In a large saucepan, bring broth to a boil. Add carrots, broccoli, mushrooms, celery, onion and garlic. Simmer, covered, for 15 minutes. Cook rotini according to package instructions. Stir rotini and chicken into soup. Heat through.

Serves 4.

Pro's Tip:
This soup tastes equally good the next day, so save the leftovers. It is called a hearty soup because of the volume of cubed chicken. This can be reduced, if you prefer a lighter soup. Substitute egg noodles for the rotini if you want a more traditional chicken noodle soup.

Casual water:
Water which accumulates where it is not meant to be (for example, ponded water from a sprinkler). A free lift no closer to the hole is allowed.

78

13. Doglegs
(Pasta)

Just when you think you've got the game of golf figured out, you discover that golf course designers are sadistic. They decide to bend fairways around lakes, rivers, forests and rock ledges, and call these elbow-shaped fairways, doglegs. Throw your guests a curve with some of these pasta delights.

Sally's Surprise Summer Salad

4 cups	dry rotini pasta	1 L
1	onion, chopped	1
1	green bell pepper, chopped	1
1	red bell pepper, chopped	1
6	cherry tomatoes, halved	6
10	medium mushrooms, sliced	10
1/2 lb.	medium Cheddar cheese, cubed	250 g
	Italian salad dressing	
	salt and lemon pepper, to taste	

Prepare rotini, ensuring that the pasta is cooked al dente. Drain, then add onion, peppers, tomatoes, mushrooms and cheese to the pasta in a large bowl. Add Italian salad dressing (you can make your own, but bottled dressing works very nicely for this type of salad). Add salt and lemon pepper to taste. Refrigerate 1 hour before serving.

Serves 4-6.

Pro's Tip:
The surprise in this recipe is the variety of ingredients that can be used. You can add just about any type of vegetable to this salad, such as broccoli, carrots, celery and even olives. For a lunchtime meal, try adding ham, salami or cubes of leftover steak.

AL DENTE:
Pasta cooked al dente means that it is tender, but firm to the bite (somewhere between the consistency of a new golf glove and the old one at the bottom of your bag!). Because different pastas take different lengths of time in their preparation, test periodically while boiling in lightly salted water. Always add a teaspoon of vegetable oil to the boiling water so the pasta will not stick.

Cannelosagne

1/2 cup	diced sweet red bell pepper	125 mL
1/2 cup	small broccoli florets	125 mL
2 tbsp.	chopped white onion	30 mL
2 cups	ricotta cheese	500 mL
1 cup	shredded Monterey Jack cheese	250 mL
10	lasagne noodles with rippled edges	10
28 oz.	can tomato sauce	796 mL

Place all vegetables in a pot of boiling water for 8 minutes. Drain. In a mixing bowl, combine the ricotta cheese, 1/2 cup (125 mL) of the shredded Monterey Jack cheese and all vegetables. Place lasagne in boiling salted water for about 10 minutes, or until al dente. Remove from heat, drain, and chill quickly with cold water. Pour tomato sauce into a 9 x 12" (23 x 30 cm) baking dish. Place 2 tbsp. (30 mL) of cheese and vegetable mixture on the end of a lasagne noodle and roll to the other end. With a serrated knife, cut rolled lasagne in half and place both halves, rippled edge up, into the tomato sauce. Continue with all remaining noodles and filling. Spread remaining Monterey Jack cheese on top and bake for 20 minutes at 375°F (190°C). Serve immediately.

Serves 4.

Pro's Tip:
For a complete meal, precede with Hale's Caesar salad. Surround the cannelosagne with meatballs and garnish with sprigs of parsley. Serve with a dry red Italian wine and crusty bread, to soak up the sauce.

Jeannie's Tortellini
with Sweet Red Peppers

8 oz. pkg.	fresh or frozen cheese tortellini	250 g pkg.
1 tbsp.	olive oil	15 mL
3	large sweet red peppers, chopped	3
2	garlic cloves, minced	2
1 tbsp.	minced onion	15 mL
1 cup	chicken broth	250 mL
1 tbsp.	tomato paste	15 mL
1/2 tsp.	thyme leaves	2 mL
dash	hot pepper sauce	dash
	freshly ground pepper	

Prepare the tortellini, ensuring that the pasta is cooked al dente. Drain and rinse with hot water. Keep warm. In a saucepan, heat the oil. Sauté the red pepper, garlic and onion for 5 minutes, or until the vegetables are tender. Add the remaining ingredients. Simmer sauce mixture for 15 minutes, or until it has thickened. Remove from heat and place in a blender. Blend until mixture is smooth. Serve immediately over tortellini.

Serves 2-4.

Pro's Tip:
Surprise your guests with this tasty red sauce (they were expecting tomato). This sauce works just as well with fish or chicken as pasta.

Nantucket Noodles
with Creamy Clammy Sauce

38	cherrystone clams	38
3 tbsp.	olive oil	45 mL
3	scallions, chopped	3
2	garlic cloves, minced	2
1 cup	sliced fresh mushrooms	250 mL
3 tbsp.	flour	45 mL
1/2 tsp.	freshly ground pepper	2 mL
1/2 tsp.	freshly ground ocean salt	2 mL
1 1/2 cups	milk	375 mL
1 1/2 cups	clam broth	375 mL
1/4 cup	dry white wine	60 mL
1/4 cup	chopped parsley	60 mL
1 lb.	fettucine noodles, cooked	454 g

Wash clams twice in separate waters. Cook rinsed clams in a pot of boiling water, adding sufficient water to cover. Reduce heat and simmer 10 minutes, or until shells open, discarding clams that remain closed. Remove clams from shells and set aside. Reserve 8 clams on the half shell for garnish. Reserve 1 1/2 cups (375 mL) of broth from the pot. Heat oil and sauté scallions, garlic and mushrooms 2 minutes. Blend in flour, pepper and salt. Slowly add milk and broth, stirring until sauce thickens. Stir in clams and remaining ingredients. Serve over fettucine noodles, cooked al dente. Garnish each plate with reserved clams on the half shell.

Serves 4.

Pro's Tips:
When you've hit so many sand traps you think you've walked across the dunes of the Cape, try this favored New England dish. Served with a bottle of dry white wine and a loaf of crusty bread.

83

Betsy's Butterflies
and Hot Sausage

1 lb.	hot Italian sausage	500 g
2 tbsp.	butter	30 mL
2 tbsp.	virgin olive oil	30 mL
1/2 cup	chopped fresh sage	125 mL
1/2 cup	chopped fresh parsley	125 mL
1	medium onion, sliced	1
3	garlic cloves, minced	3
2 cups	chicken stock	500 mL
1 lb.	dry butterfly pasta	500 g
2 cups	mozzarella cheese in 1/2" (1.3 cm) cubes	500 mL
	salt and pepper, to taste	

In a saucepan, cover sausage with water and bring to a boil. Reduce heat and simmer about 10 minutes, until sausage is fully cooked. Remove sausage and allow to dry a few minutes. Cut into 1/4" (1 cm) slices. In a large pan, combine 1 tbsp. (15 mL) butter, olive oil, sage and parsley. Cook over medium heat for 2 minutes. Set aside sage, parsley mixture in a bowl. Add remaining butter, onion and garlic to the pan, cooking for 4 minutes. Add chicken stock over high heat. Bring to a boil and reduce to 1 cup (250 mL), which will take about 10 minutes. In another large pot, add pasta to boiling salted water and cook until al dente. Drain water and return pasta to pot. Add the reduced stock, sausage and mozzarella cheese cubes. Season with salt and pepper to taste. Transfer to a large platter, sprinkling sautéed sage and parsley over the top.

Serves 6.

Pro's Tip:
White brick cheese can be substituted for mozzarella. Should be served with a full-bodied red wine and thickly sliced Italian bread.

84

14. Scrambles
(Eggs)

A scramble is a friendly tournament format where teams of four play the best ball. Speaking of scrambles, how about trying some of these egg-sighting brunch suggestions. What better way to start the day.

Shrimp and Scrambled Eggs on Pumpernickel

2	eggs	2
1 tbsp.	heavy cream (35% butterfat)	15 mL
	salt and pepper, to taste	
	Worcestershire sauce, to taste	
4 tsp.	butter	20 mL
1/4 cup	cooked small salad shrimp	60 mL
1	slice pumpernickel bread	1
1 tbsp.	finely chopped fresh dill	15 mL

Beat the eggs with the cream, salt, pepper and Worcestershire sauce. Melt 1 tbsp. (15 mL) butter in a frying pan. Pour in the egg mixture and cook over low heat until set. As soon as the eggs begin to set, add the shrimp, stirring so the mixture doesn't stick. Toast the bread and lightly spread with butter; cover with the shrimp and eggs and, finally, sprinkle dill over the top.

Serves 1.

Pro's Tip:
This recipe is too magnificent to eat alone. Double it and share with your golfing partner.

Skins game:
When 3 or 4 golfers playing together wager on skins, 1 player must have the lowest score on the hole alone to win the skin. If 2 tie with the lowest score, then all have tied, and the wager is carried on until 1 person wins the skin.

Fran's Fresh Baked Eggs

4	large ripe tomatoes	4
	salt and freshly ground pepper, to taste	
1/4 cup	basil leaves	60 mL
4	eggs	4
2 tsp.	white wine vinegar	10 mL
1 tbsp.	olive oil	15 mL

Slice off the tops of the tomatoes below the stem. Scoop out pulp and seeds, leaving a hollowed bowl. Sprinkle the insides of the tomato bowl with salt and pepper. Purée the tomato pulp and tops in a food processor or blender. Place the tomato shells in an oven-safe dish and break an egg into each one. Place a whole basil leaf on top of each egg white. Bake in a preheated 350°F (180°C) oven for 20 minutes, or until the eggs have set. Chop the remaining basil and stir into the tomato purée. Add the white wine vinegar and olive oil, adding salt and pepper to taste. Place the tomato shells on separate plates, then pour the sauce over each, allowing excess sauce to pool around the base of tomato on plate.

Serves 4.

Pro's Tip:
Start with tomatoes at room temperature. Trust the cooking time with this recipe. The egg doesn't cook until the last few minutes. For a special breakfast or brunch, this makes a great centrepiece. Draws the same raves as a double eagle.

87

Benedict's Eggs

11	eggs	11
2 tbsp.	lemon juice	30 mL
	salt	
1 pinch	white pepper	1 pinch
	butter	
8	thin slices Black Forest-style ham	8
4	English muffins	4
	chopped parsley or chives	
	freshly ground pepper, to taste	

First, prepare the Hollandaise sauce; place 3 egg yolks, lemon juice, salt and white pepper into a blender. Melt 1/2 cup (125 mL) butter in a microwave, placing in a microwave-safe dish and putting on high for 25 seconds, or until foaming. Blend the yolk mixture in a blender at top speed for 3 seconds. Remove cover and pour the hot butter into the blender, first drop by drop, then in a small stream. Set the blender jar with the completed Hollandaise sauce in lukewarm water until ready to use. In a skillet, fry the ham slices until they are cooked through and are slightly brown. Split 4 English muffins and toast them under the broiler. Butter lightly. In a large skillet, poach 8 eggs in salted boiling water. Top each of the toasted muffin halves with a slice of ham, an egg and a coating of Hollandaise sauce. Add salt and pepper to taste and top with chopped parsley or chives.

Serves 4.

Pro's Tip:
Reheating the Hollandaise sauce usually will cause curdling, so prepare close to actual serving time.

Mike's Mushroom
and Cheese Omelet

4 tbsp.	butter	60 mL
1/2	medium onion, diced	1/2
3/4 cup	chopped fresh mushrooms	175 mL
6	eggs	6
2 tbsp.	milk	30 mL
3/4 cup	shredded medium Cheddar cheese	175 mL
	salt and pepper, to taste	
1	wedge lemon	1

In a skillet, heat 2 tbsp. (30 mL) butter and sauté onions and sliced mushrooms until vegetables are limp. Remove from heat and set aside. Beat the eggs until well mixed and slightly frothy. Add milk and mix thoroughly. In a 10" (25 cm) frying pan over medium heat, melt the remaining butter. Tip the pan so that the bottom and part way up the sides are completely coated. Add egg mixture to pan. Working quickly, shake the pan with your left hand. Using a fork in your right hand, stir the eggs all around, then a few times in the middle. Stroke the mixture to the center of the pan. When the edges of the omelet appear to be cooked, spread the shredded cheese, onions and mushrooms over the top. Sprinkle with salt, pepper and a few drops of lemon juice. Fold over about 1/3 of the omelet from one edge, then fold over 1/3 from the opposite edge. Continue cooking until egg is cooked to a slightly golden hue. Flip omelet onto a plate, divide, then enjoy.

Serves 4.

Pro's Tip:
Don't be afraid to experiment with omelets. Use olives, hot or sweet peppers, bacon, ham, or any other favorite taste treat to create your own masterpiece.

Sam's Cheesy Super Soufflé

4 tbsp.	butter	60 mL
4 tbsp.	all-purpose flour	60 mL
1/2 tsp.	salt	2 mL
1/2 tsp.	dry mustard	2 mL
1 dash	cayenne pepper	1 dash
1 cup	milk	250 mL
2 cups	shredded Cheddar cheese	500 mL
4	eggs, separated	4
	Fresh Mushroom Sauce (see page 58)	

In a saucepan, melt the butter. Add flour, salt, mustard and cayenne pepper, mixing thoroughly. Add milk. Cook over medium heat until thickened and bubbly, stirring constantly. Reduce the heat to low and add the cheese to the sauce mixture. Stir until all cheese has melted. Remove the mixture from heat. In a mixing bowl, beat the egg yolks until they are thick and slightly frothy. Gradually add the cheese mixture, mixing thoroughly. Cool the mixture for 5 minutes. In a separate mixing bowl, beat the egg whites until they form stiff peaks. Gradually pour the yolk mixture into the whites. Fold the mixture until it has been evenly distributed. Pour the completed mixture into an ungreased 2-quart (2 L) soufflé dish. Bake in a 300°F (150°C) oven for 50 minutes, or until a knife inserted off-center comes out clean. Serve the soufflé immediately, with Fresh Mushroom Sauce.

Serves 4.

Pro's Tip:
To create the fancy "top hat" look on your soufflé, trace a circle through the batter after you pour it in the soufflé dish, approximately 1" (2.5 cm) from the edge of the dish and 1" (2.5 cm) deep.

15. Putting Out
(Desserts)

One of the oldest adages in golf is that you drive for show but you putt for dough. Almost half of the strokes in a round occur with your ball already on the putting surface. Nothing is more satisfying than finishing a hole with a great putt, and the same can be said for finishing a meal with a great dessert.

Stuffed Montego Bay Bananas

1/4 cup	raisins	60 mL
	dark Caribbean rum	
3	large bananas	3
1	lemon, juice of	1
1/2 cup	butter, softened	125 mL
1/2 cup	finely ground sugar (berry sugar)	125 mL
4 tbsp.	mixture of chopped almonds and cashews	60 mL
	maraschino cherries	

Marinate the raisins in 2 tbsp. (30 mL) rum for 1/2 hour in the refrigerator. Peel the bananas and cut lengthwise. Brush with lemon juice so they will not darken too quickly. In a medium bowl, blend the softened butter and sugar together, then add 2 tbsp. (30 mL) rum. Fold in the almonds and cashews. Hollow out a 1/2" (1.3 cm) deep cavity in the bananas. Spoon in the sugar-butter mixture, leveling off the top. Cover with the raisins and any leftover rum marinade. Garnish with maraschino cherries.

Serves 3.

Pro's Tip:
This may be the most decadently delicious recipe in the whole book. It defies improvement. Don't even think about whipped cream! No problem, mon.

Brandied Peaches

19 oz.	can sliced peaches in their syrup	540 mL
1/4 cup	brown sugar	60 mL
2 tbsp.	butter	30 mL
1/2 tsp.	cinnamon powder	3 mL
1/2 tsp.	lemon juice	3 mL
1 1/2 oz.	brandy	45 mL

In a large saucepan, mix all ingredients well. Heat over medium heat, stirring occasionally until boiling. Lower the heat and simmer a further 5 minutes.

Serves 4.

Pro's Tip:
Served over French Vanilla ice cream, this is guaranteed to close your eyes and make you dream sensational thoughts. Savor it, as you would a 300-yard drive.

Enough club:
Under the circumstances of distance, wind conditions, hazards, to name a few, what would the appropriate club befor the shot? If the 8 iron was "not enough club" and came up short of the green, it might have been wiser to use the 7 or 6 iron for enough club.

Fresh Fruit and Biscuit Ring

1 pkg.	ready-to-prepare refrigerated buttermilk biscuits	1 pkg.
1 tbsp.	olive oil	15 mL
2 tbsp.	grated Parmesan cheese	30 mL
2 tsp.	dried parsley	10 mL
1/4 cup	dry white wine	60 mL
2 cups	fresh fruit (suggest melons, strawberries, and mandarin orange slices)	500 mL

Place the buttermilk biscuits in a ring shape on a greased cookie sheet, sides touching. Drizzle the tops with olive oil. Sprinkle the cheese and parsley over the tops of the biscuits. Heat oven to 400°F (200°C) and bake the ring for 10 minutes, or until the biscuits have turned a golden brown. To serve, place the biscuit ring on a serving plate. Mix the wine and fruit together in a bowl, then place in a fancy serving dish in the middle of the ring.

Serves 4.

Pro's Tip:
Perhaps the toughest part of this recipe is finding a solid piece of Parmesan cheese to grate. However, this makes a nice dessert to follow a spicy chili or other hot foods.

__First rule of__ golf is never putt a gimme. If your opponent thinks it is that easy, don't humiliate yourself by missing it.

Debbie's 18th Green Grasshopper Pie

2 cups	finely crushed dark chocolate cookie crumbs	500 mL
1/4 cup	butter or margarine, melted	60 mL
8 oz.	cream cheese, softened	250 g
10 oz.	can sweetened condensed milk	284 mL
6 tbsp.	lemon juice	90 mL
1/4 cup	green crème de menthe	60 mL
1/4 cup	white crème de cacao	60 mL
1 cup	heavy cream (35% butterfat), stiffly whipped	250 mL

Combine crumbs and butter. Press firmly on bottom and up sides of a buttered 9" (23 cm) pie plate. Allow to chill for 15 minutes. In a large mixer bowl, beat cheese until fluffy. Gradually beat in condensed milk until smooth. Stir in lemon juice and liqueurs. Fold in the whipped cream. Chill 20 minutes. Gently pour into crust. Refrigerate or freeze for 4 hours, or until set. Leftovers, if any, may be refrigerated or frozen.

Serves 6.

Recipe pictured opposite page 96.

Pro's Tip:
Although the color and aroma shout out "Taste me," the pie can be further enhanced by garnishing with fresh mint leaves or chocolate shavings.

Added Attraction: Form the crust into a kidney-shaped golf green, on a large platter. Mound the green pie filling over the crust and garnish with a home-made pin.

Sue's Scrumptious Butter Tarts

1/2 cup	chopped walnuts	125 mL
12	prepared tart shells	12
1/2 cup	brown sugar	125 mL
1/2 cup	corn syrup	125 mL
1/4 cup	softened butter	60 mL
1	egg, beaten	1
1 tsp.	vanilla	5 mL
1/4 tsp.	salt	1 mL

Place the walnuts in the bottom of the tart shells. Mix remaining ingredients thoroughly in a bowl. Fill each tart shell 2/3 full with the sugar mixture. Bake on the bottom level of a preheated oven at 425°F (220°C) for 12 minutes, or until the tarts are set. Be careful not to overbake. Cool tarts, then remove from pans.

Pro's Tip:
Butter tarts taste exceptionally good ranging in temperature from just warm from the oven to frozen (great with piping hot coffee), depending on personal taste. You can substitute raisins for the nuts in this recipe.

You know you've got your temper under control when you swear only once after 4 putting.

16. Duffers Delight
(Barbecue)

Golf is like sex: When it is good, it's great; and when it's bad, it is still pretty good. Just as you don't have to be a professional to enjoy the game of golf, you don't have to be a French chef to cook a good meal. Even the simplest backyard barbecue can make you a hero.

Chickeyburgers

2 lbs.	ground chicken or turkey	1 kg
1	egg, lightly beaten	1
2 tbsp.	barbecue sauce	30 mL
1/2 cup	dry bread crumbs	125 mL
1 tbsp.	chopped fresh basil	15 mL
1 tbsp.	chopped fresh oregano	15 mL
1 tbsp.	chopped fresh parsley	15 mL
1 tsp.	seasoned salt	5 mL
1/2 tsp.	ground black pepper	2 mL
2 tbsp.	finely chopped onion	30 mL
8	burger buns	8

Combine all ingredients, except buns, in a bowl, then form into 8 burger patties. Barbecue or fry on medium heat for about 12 minutes. Burgers made from poultry take slightly longer to cook than beef, and must be cooked to a minimum 156°F (70°C). Serve on lightly toasted burger buns.

Serves 8.

Pro's Tip:
Ground poultry should be used within 2 days of being ground. It cooks to a lighter color than the traditional beef hamburger, so don't be fooled into thinking it must be browned like a beef burger.

*A **movie title** that describes many golf games: The Good, The Bad and The Ugly.*

Juney's Juicy Beefy Burgers

1 1/2 lbs.	lean ground beef	750 g
2	garlic cloves, minced	2
1 tbsp.	minced onion	15 mL
1	egg	1
1/4 cup	oat bran or dried bread crumbs	60 mL
1 tbsp.	Worcestershire sauce	15 mL
1/2 tsp.	seasoned salt	2 mL
4	large hamburger buns	4
	toppings to taste	

In a mixing bowl, combine all ingredients, except buns and toppings, and mix thoroughly. Form into 4 tightly bound round patties. Squeeze patty edges with fingertips, creating wavy indentations. Cook over a medium-hot barbecue for 5 minutes, flip, then continue until meat is cooked as desired. Lightly toast buns on the edge of the barbecue. Place burgers on buns and top to taste with slices of cheese, sliced tomatoes, sweet cucumber relish, mustard, sliced Spanish onion rings, shredded lettuce, mayonnaise and lengthwise-sliced dill pickles.

Pro's Tip:
As an additional topping, while barbecue is warming, combine 1 diced onion, 6 sliced mushrooms, 1 tsp. (5 mL) Worcestershire sauce and 1 tbsp. (15 mL) butter; wrap in aluminum foil. Place on barbecue grill for 10 minutes and serve hot on your burgers.

A good golfer can often be judged by his number of divorces.

Bernie's Burning Pork Burgers

1	egg	1
1/4 cup	oat bran or bread crumbs	60 mL
1/4 cup	finely chopped onion	60 mL
1-2	garlic cloves, minced	1-2
1 tsp.	fennel seed	5 mL
	red pepper flakes, to taste	
1/2 tsp.	salt	2 mL
1/2 tsp.	dried thyme	2 mL
	pepper, to taste	
2 tbsp.	water	30 mL
1 lb.	lean ground pork	500 g
	toppings, to taste	

In a bowl, beat the egg. Add oat bran, onion, garlic, fennel seed, salt, thyme, pepper and 1/2 tsp. (2 mL) red pepper flakes or more for a more burning taste. Mix thoroughly; shape into 4 evenly sized patties. Cook the patties on a hot barbecue for 5 minutes. Flip and cook for an additional 10 minutes, or until the patties are cooked through. Add toppings, to taste.

Serves 4.

Pro's Tip:
For a bit more "burn," consider adding a dash of Tabasco sauce, or a finely chopped jalapeño pepper. Make it as hot as you dare for your foursome.

Calvin's Citrus Zest Pork Chops

1	orange, juice of	1
1	lemon, juice of	1
1 tsp.	grated orange rind	5 mL
1 tsp.	grated lemon rind	5 mL
2 tbsp.	olive oil	30 mL
2 tbsp.	minced green onions	30 mL
3/4 tsp.	chili powder	4 mL
1/4 tsp.	paprika	2 mL
	freshly ground pepper	
1/4 tsp.	hot pepper sauce	2 mL
4 x 6 oz.	loin pork chops	4 x 170 g
	salt, to taste	

In a shallow container large enough to fit all of the pork chops, mix together the juices, rinds, oil, green onion, chili powder, paprika, 1/4 tsp. (2 mL) freshly ground pepper and hot pepper sauce. Place the pork chops in the marinade; turn over to coat both sides. Cover and refrigerate at least 8 hours. Remove the chops, reserving any leftover marinade. Cook the chops on the barbecue over a medium-high setting; turn after 5 minutes, brush with the remaining marinade, then continue cooking for an additional 7-10 minutes, or until no longer pink. Season with salt and additional freshly ground pepper to taste.

Serves 4.

Recipe pictured opposite page 96.

Pro's Tip:
To add additional color to this dish, cover the chops with a very thin slice of orange after they have been turned and brushed with marinade.

101

Lee's Round Dogs with Salsa

4	jumbo wieners	4
1 cup	hot salsa	250 mL
4	soft Kaiser rolls	4

In order to cook the wieners properly, they must be scored with a continuous diagonal cut around the wiener from one end to the other. The cut marks should be 1/2" (1.3 cm) apart. Using toothpicks, secure the ends together, making a circle. Cook the wieners on a barbecue until they are blistered and heated through. Slice and toast the Kaiser rolls on the edge of the barbecue. Remove from heat when slightly browned. Place a wiener circle on the bun; spoon desired amount of salsa into the middle of the circle. Cover with remaining bun halves.

Serves 4.

Recipe pictured opposite page 48.

Pro's Tip:
This recipe tastes great. To add more pizzazz, slice a Spanish onion into rings and fry in butter until the onions are tender, adding freshly ground pepper to taste. Use this and grated Cheddar cheese as a final topping to your round dogs.

Definition of 1 wood:
The Big Kahuna. This loosely translated means "club that sends ball into rough, woods or trench."

102

17. The Junior Program
(Junior Cooks)

Most clubs design programs which encourage junior golfers to understand and learn the game. The following recipes encourage the juniors in your household with tasty and nutritious meals which they can prepare themselves.

Egg Pizzaomelette

2	eggs	2
1 tbsp.	milk	15 mL
1 tbsp.	butter	15 mL
6	green pepper rings	6
6	onion rings	6
	pizza sauce (tomato sauce with oregano, basil and red pepper flakes)	
1/3 cup	shredded mozzarella cheese	75 mL
	pepperoni or cooked sausage, thinly sliced	

Beat eggs with milk. In a frying pan over medium heat, melt butter and lightly sauté the green pepper rings and onion rings for 2 minutes, or until tender. Remove and reserve. Add the beaten egg to the same frying pan. When the egg is no longer runny in the middle, spread a thin layer of tomato sauce over the inner 2/3 of the egg. Garnish with the shredded cheese and sausage. Top with the reserved onions and peppers. Cover the pan for another minute, until cheese has melted. Remove to a plate and serve immediately.

Serves 1.

Pro's Tip:
This is a great family brunch creation for after that early Sunday morning round.

Dawn's Sunrise Muffins

1	English muffin	1
	butter	
1	egg	1
1	slice ham	1
1	slice processed cheese	1

Slice muffin in half and toast. Butter lightly. Place 1 tsp. (5 mL) butter in the bottom of a microwave-safe coffee mug. Gently drop egg into the mug. Break the yolk by piercing lightly with a fork. Cover the mug loosely with a piece of microwave-safe plastic wrap. Place in microwave and cook on high for 50 seconds. Remove cup from microwave. Cover 1 slice of muffin with the slice of ham. Cover the other half with the processed cheese. Place both halves in the microwave and cook on high for 25 seconds, or until the cheese has completely softened. Remove the egg from the cup and place on the cheese half of the muffin. Cover the egg with the ham-covered muffin slice.

Serves 1.

Pro's Tip:
Since this is a great kid's meal; let them experiment with variations. Consider using tomato slices or hot dog slices instead of the ham. Try gently beating the egg with 1 tbsp.(15 mL) of milk before placing it in the cup for microwaving.

Jumbo's Bacon and Apple Franks

6	jumbo hot dog wieners	6
1/2 cup	shredded Cheddar or mozzarella cheese	125 mL
2	apples	2
	cinnamon, to taste	
12	bacon strips	12

Slice wieners lengthwise, almost through, opening to create a wide trough. Spread a thin layer of shredded cheese in bottom of the trough. Peel and core the apples, then dice into 1/4" (1 cm) chunks, placing them over the cheese and pressing down firmly. Sprinkle cinnamon powder over the apple. Wrap each stuffed wiener with bacon, using 1 or 2 slices as needed, and hold in place with toothpicks. Place all 6 wrapped wieners in an oven pan and cook in oven at 375°F (190°C) for 20 minutes, or until crispness of the bacon meets your satisfaction. Serve on a bun or with potato skins.

Serves 6.

Pro's Tip:
To reduce the overall cooking time, microwave the bacon on a paper towel for 90 seconds before wrapping the wieners. And by all means, don't forget to remove the toothpicks before you bite in.

***The odds of** an amateur golfer making a hole in one is over 12,000 to 1.*

106

Beef Torpedoes

1 lb.	medium ground beef	500 g
1	medium onion, chopped	1
1/2	green pepper, chopped	1/2
1/4 cup	chopped celery	60 mL
3/4 cup	tomato ketchup	175 mL
1/4 cup	water	60 mL
1 tbsp.	brown sugar	15 mL
1 tbsp.	lemon juice	15 mL
1 tbsp.	Worcestershire sauce	15 mL
4	crusty bread rolls, about 10" (25cm) long	4

In a frying pan over medium heat, cook the beef, onion, green pepper and celery until meat is no longer pink and the vegetables have softened. Spoon off all the fat and juice from the pan. Add the tomato ketchup, water, brown sugar, lemon juice and Worcestershire sauce to the pan. Raise heat until the mixture begins to boil, then reduce heat, simmering, uncovered, about 5 minutes, until the mixture begins to thicken. Cut off a slice of the bread crust lengthwise, about 1/4 of the bread's thickness. Hollow out the bread by removing some of the inner dough, making a trough. Spoon the barbecue-flavored beef mixture into the bread. Replace the top half for serving.

Serves 4.

Recipe pictured opposite page 48.

Pro's Tip:
For a speedier sandwich, simply add your favorite prepared barbecue sauce to the cooked meat and vegetable mixture. Try adding shredded cheese and lettuce either above or below the meat filling.

107

Chip's Chocolate Monster Cookies

1 cup	all-purpose flour	250 mL
1/2 tsp.	baking soda	2 mL
1/2 tsp.	salt	2 mL
1/2 cup	margarine or butter	125 mL
3/4 cup	sugar (brown and white combined)	175 mL
1/2 tsp.	vanilla extract	2 mL
1	egg	1
6 oz.	chocolate chips	170 g

In a bowl, combine flour, baking soda and salt. Set this aside. In a second bowl, blend together the margarine, sugar and vanilla. Beat in the egg. Gradually add the flour mixture. When it is well mixed, add the chocolate chips. Preheat oven to 375°F (190°C). On a large ungreased cookie sheet, place 3 tbsp. (45 mL) of batter for each cookie, about 5" (13 cm) apart. Lightly flatten the batter, allowing it to spread evenly. Place 1 cookie sheet at a time in the oven on the middle rack for 10 minutes, until the cookies are lightly browned and are about 6" (15 cm) across.

Pro's Tip:
This recipe is so easy. Stay out of the kitchen and let the kids do it all by themselves (including the cleanup).

Food for thought:
The odds of hitting your shot into the water increase with the number of old balls you could have used.

18. The Professional World Tour
(International Specialties)

 Golf is a game enjoyed worldwide. Every country is famous for at least one good course, be it golf or food.

Venetian White Pizza

1/2 cup	halved fresh scallops	125 mL
1/2 cup	shelled and deveined raw medium shrimp	125 mL
14"	flatbread pizza base (purchased)	35 cm
3 tbsp.	olive oil	45 mL
3	plum tomatoes, sliced	3
1	small zucchini, sliced	1
1	green pepper, cut into rings	1
6 oz.	smoked salmon	170 g
1/2 cup	shredded mozzarella cheese	125 mL
	herb and spice mixture of finely chopped fresh oregano, basil, parsley, dillweed, freshly ground pepper and garlic powder	
1	shallot or spring onion, diced	1

Place the scallops and shrimp on a microwave-safe dish. Cook in the microwave on high for 2 minutes. Brush the pizza base with olive oil. Arrange the tomato slices, zucchini and green pepper rings in a circular fashion on the pizza base to completely cover it. Lightly brush scallops and shrimp with oil and arrange on top of vegetables. Cut smoked salmon into 1" (2.5 cm) squares, roll into tubes, then arrange on top of pizza. Sprinkle cheese, herb mixture and onion over top. Bake in oven according to pizza base directions, making sure the cheese does not burn. Serve immediately.

Serves 4.

Recipe pictured opposite page 80.

The Madrid Omelet

2	large potatoes	2
3 tbsp.	vegetable oil	45 mL
1	medium onion, coarsely chopped	1
6	fresh eggs	6
	salt and pepper, to taste	

Peel the potatoes and cut them into 1/4" (1 cm) cubes. Wash and drain. In a skillet, heat 2 tbsp. (30 mL) oil, fry the onions and potatoes over medium heat. Stir the vegetables frequently, cooking them until the potatoes have softened and are starting to brown, about 20 minutes. In a bowl, beat the 6 eggs, adding salt and pepper to taste. Transfer the vegetables from the pan into the egg mixture. Drain off as much oil as possible and, leaving as little oil as possible in the pan, return the vegetable and egg mixture, flattening it with a spatula or fork. Cook for about 5 minutes, lifting the edges occasionally to allow the liquid egg to run under. Place a large plate over the pan; invert the pan and plate to flip the omelet upside down. Slide the omelet back into the pan and cook a further 5 minutes, until it has browned. Serve on a large plate, dividing the omelet into 4 portions.

Serves 4.

Pro's Tip:
A mimosa, equal parts freshly squeezed orange juice and champagne, accompanies this dish well. This is the very simple and basic Spanish omelet. Great additions to this include mushrooms, parsley, chopped ham, anchovies or cooked sausage.

Parisian Frog Legs

48	single frog legs	48
1/2 cup	white wine vinegar	125 mL
1/2 cup	water	125 mL
	flour, seasoned with salt, paprika and garlic powder	
3/4 cup	butter	175 mL
6	garlic cloves, minced	6
1 cup	heavy cream (35% butterfat)	250 mL
	salt and pepper, to taste	
	lemon wedges	
	chopped parsley	

Marinate the frog legs in white wine vinegar and water for 1 hour. Remove and dry with a paper towel. Coat the dried legs with the flour mixture. In a large frying pan, melt 1/4 cup (60 mL) of butter. Slowly sauté all the legs for 20 minutes, turning frequently. Cook until frog legs are a golden brown color. Arrange on a large platter. Melt the remaining butter in another frying pan. Sauté the garlic for 60 seconds at medium heat, as butter starts to darken. Stir in the heavy cream. Continue heating and stirring until the sauce starts to thicken. Add a dash of salt and pepper. Pour over the frog legs. Garnish with lemon wedges and chopped parsley.

Serves 4.

Pro's Tip:
A dry white French wine is as obligatory for this meal as putting out every hole in a tournament. A warning with this meal; your guests may be apprehensive about eating frog legs. Don't joke about catching them at the side of the lake on the fifth hole.

London Broil Roast

1 cup	dry red wine	250 mL
1/4 cup	oil	60 mL
1/2 tsp.	salt	2 mL
1/2 tsp.	pepper	2 mL
1 1/2 lbs.	flank steak	675 g
1/2 lb.	ground veal	227 g
1/2 lb.	ground pork	227 g
1/2 tsp.	red pepper flakes	2 mL
1/2 tsp.	fennel seed	2 mL
1/4 tsp.	garlic salt	1 mL

Prepare a marinade with wine, oil, salt and pepper. Pierce flank steak with a fork about 50 times on each side. Place steak in marinade for 1 hour, turning occasionally. Combine veal, pork, red pepper flakes, fennel seed and garlic salt, mixing well. Remove steak from marinade and lay flat, covering evenly with the veal and pork mixture. Roll up the steak and tie with kitchen string. Place in a roasting pan. Cook in preheated oven at 325°F (160°C) for 1 hour, until firm. Periodically, during cooking, baste with reserved marinade. Remove from oven, allow to sit 10 minutes. To serve, slice into 1" (2.5 cm) thick portions.

Serves 4.

Pro's Tip:
The London broil is suitably applied to the barbecue as a steak. Preslice the marinated flank steak into 1" (2.5 cm) strips and wrap around the veal and pork mixture shaped like hamburger patties. Surround the steak with a slice of bacon secured with toothpicks. Position a 1" (2.5 cm) cube of steak in the middle of each pattie. Barbecue over medium heat until veal and pork mixture is cooked, about 8 minutes each side. Round steak can be substituted for flank steak.

Cozumel Seafood Tortillas

1 1/2 cups	cornmeal	375 mL
1 1/2 cups	flour	375 mL
2	eggs	2
2 cups	milk	500 mL
	salt	
	vegetable oil	
2	avocados	2
1/2 lb.	medium shrimp, shelled and cooked	250 mL
1/2 lb.	cooked creab meat, flaked	250 mL
	freshly chopped parsley	
1	lemon	1
2	egg whites	2

To make the tortillas, whisk together the cornmeal and flour. Stir in the 2 whole eggs, milk and 1/2 tsp. (2 mL) salt, whisking the mixture into a smooth batter. Lightly oil a nonstick frying pan and heat to a setting slightly higher than medium. Pour 2 tbsp. (30 mL) of batter in pan, swirling pan so batter cooks in a round shape. Cook just 1 minute on each side, then lay on a paper towel until all tortillas are cooked. Set aside and keep warm. For the filling, peel and mash the avocados. Blend in the shrimp, crab, parsley, 2 tbsp. (30 mL) of freshly squeezed lemon juice and a dash of salt. Place the filling on 1/2 of each tortilla shell. Paint the edges of the tortilla crust with egg white. Fold the shell over the filling and press the edges to seal the filling inside. Briefly sauté the tortilla in a mixture of butter and oil. Serve hot.

Serves 4.

Pro's Tip:
Now that you know how to make the tortilla shells, only your imagination limits the flavor combinations that you can enjoy. Cerveza, por favor.

114

19. The 19th Hole

The 19th is the one water hole that no one avoids. It is the place for your foursome to relax, say "if only I had..." at least a dozen times, and no matter how bad your round, make plans for your next game.

Summery Sangria

4 oz.	orange liqueur	125 mL
4 oz.	brandy	125 mL
50 oz.	dry white wine	1.5 L
1/2 cup	sugar	125 mL
25 oz.	cold soda water	750 mL
	strawberries, orange slices,	
	pitted plums, melon balls	

In a large glass pitcher, combine orange liqueur, brandy, wine and sugar. Pour 2 parts of this with 1 part of soda water into a tall glass filled with fruits and ice cubes. No need to mix ice cubes into the pitcher, they'll only water down the liquor mixture. Keep pitcher in cooler until served.

Serves 12-15.

Recipe pictured opposite page 16.

19th Hole:
The only hole where golfers are happy to be in the drink and never complain about the number of shots they took.

116

Barbados Party Rum Punch

1/3 cup	sugar	75 mL
1/3 cup	warm water	75 mL
1/2 cup	lemon juice	125 mL
1/2 cup	grapefruit juice	125 mL
1 2/3 cups	unsweetened pineapple juice	400 mL
3 cups	Barbados rum	750 mL
4 cups	club soda	1 L
	fruit for garnish	

Dissolve sugar in warm water. In a large punch bowl, combine all of the ingredients, except the garnish. Garnish punch bowl with slices of fruit. Serve punch in a highball glass over cracked ice (the more ice, the better!).

Serves 12-15.

Pro's Tip:
Rum punch is made using the following simple formula: 1 part sour, 2 parts sweet, 3 parts strong, 4 parts weak. Experiment with various juices and sodas. Develop the combination that reminds you of warm sandy beaches on an island in the sun.

No putt was *ever longer or drive shorter than one that was bet upon.*

Champagne Punch

12 1/2 oz.	can frozen concentrated fruit punch, thawed	355 mL
12 1/2 oz.	can frozen concentrated limeade, thawed	355 mL
1 1/2 cups	vodka	375 mL
26 oz.	bottle chilled club soda	750 mL
26 oz.	bottle chilled champagne fruit garnish, optional	750 mL

In a large punch bowl, combine the fruit punch, limeade and vodka. Chill. When ready to serve, add the club soda and champagne. Keep punch chilled by adding an ice ring. Garnish punch bowl with orange slices and fresh strawberries, if available. Use a cocktail glass or champagne flute for serving.

Serves 12.

Pro's Tip:
Make an ice ring by filling an empty plastic margarine container with water and placing a round item like a salt shaker in the middle. Blend a few drops of food coloring for effect. Place in freezer until hard and pop out. Other molds include a bundt pan, angel food cake pan, or gelatin mold. For added effect, you can also add whole strawberries, blueberries, sliced peaches, etc., to the ice ring mold before freezing.

Best tip of the day:
What you give your caddy who has had the eyes of a hawk, the patience of a soldier and the memory of a Mafia witness.

118

Cranberry Punch

8 cups	chilled cranberry punch	2 L
26 oz.	bottle vodka	750 mL
2 cups	chilled ginger ale	500 mL
2 cups	chilled club soda	500 mL
	fruit for garnish	

Mix all the above ingredients, except garnish, in a large punch bowl. Add a ring of ice to keep punch chilled. Garnish the punch bowl with various fruit slices.

Serves 12-15.

Pro's Tip:
All of the punches in the 19th hole have fruit recommended as garnish. In all cases, the fruit only adds to the color and beauty of the presentation. For only a few minutes work, you will impress your guests and have them believing you fussed for hours.

__Old golfers never__ die; they just lose their drive.

119

Yuletide Eggnog

3	eggs, separated	3
3/4 cup	sugar	175 mL
1/4 tsp.	salt	1 mL
2 3/4 cups	milk	675 mL
1 1/4 cups	heavy cream (35% butterfat)	300 mL
1 tbsp.	vanilla extract	15 mL
1 cup	spiced rum	250 mL
	grated nutmeg	

In a large mixing bowl, beat the egg yolks. Add 1/2 cup (125 mL) of sugar and the salt; continue beating. Gradually add the milk and cream. Stirring constantly, cook the egg yolk mixture over boiling water until it has thickened to a consistency that will coat a spoon. Remove from the heat and cool. Add the vanilla extract, then chill. Beat the egg whites until stiff. Gradually add the remaining sugar, beating constantly until stiff. Fold the beaten egg white mixture into the chilled custard mixture. Refrigerate. When you are ready to serve, pour the chilled eggnog into a punch bowl and add the rum. Sprinkle nutmeg over the top. Serve immediately.

Serves 10.

Pro's Tip:

Spiced rum is made by at least 1 major distillery and is available at most liquor stores. For the eggnog, add a tray of ice cubes to the punchbowl; it helps keep the eggnog nicely chilled and makes it go a little farther too.

Index

121

122

123

From The Golf Course . . . To The Main Course

SCORE CARD	1 Practice Tee	2 Sandtraps	3 Greens	4 Hooks	5 Slices	6 Birdies	7 The Mulligan	8 The Hot Round	9 Playing in Rough
EAGLE (Fantastic)									
BIRDIE (Terrific)									
PAR (Delicious)									
BOGEY (Average)									

From The Golf Course . . . To The Main Course

SCORE CARD	**10** The Turn	**11** Chip Shots	**12** Water Hazards	**13** Doglegs	**14** Scrambles	**15** Putting Out	**16** Duffer's Delight	**17** Junior Program	**18** World Tour
EAGLE (Fantastic)									
BIRDIE (Terrific)									
PAR (Delicious)									
BOGEY (Average)									

About Our Foursome

GREG PARKER has spent a decade in the food industry, developing and marketing new products, and presently manages a chicken processing business. As comfortable in the kitchen as on the golf course, Greg and his wife Debbie love to entertain unsuspecting guests with trial recipes. Although the golfer's cookbook was conceptualized by Greg in 1982, it was not until 1993 that he and Rob collaborated to complete the venture.

ROB FOSTER is a senior systems analyst, designing computer software for the business group of a major newspaper chain. Outside of work, Rob is an active sports enthusiast and political organizer, but still reserves time with his wife Sue to pursue their culinary endeavors. His talents for writing and computer formatting were an essential combination required to put this book together. He and Greg are already testing and saving recipes for a future cookbook.

DAN MALSTROM is a full-time graphic artist. His many talents are displayed in a variety of media, from illustrations for books and newspapers to painting ceiling murals in public centers. His versatility runs from caricatures to water colors and fine art. Dan's line drawings throughout the book humorously merge the concepts of golfing and cooking in his own unique fashion.

BRUNO RUBERTO has been in the newspaper industry for 16 years, starting as a reporter, and is now an advertising features editor. This is the third time that Bruno has tackled the entire layout design for a book. He also edited and published the first two. Highly skilled in computer enhance design, he accepted the challenge of this book and produced exceptional results.

Share *From the Golf Course to the Main Course*
with your golfing partners

Order at $12.95 per book
plus $3.00 (total order) for shipping and handling

Number of books _____ x $12.95 $ _____

Shipping and handling $ 3.00

Subtotal $ _____

In Canada, add 7% GST (Subtotal x .07) $ _____

Total Enclosed $ _____

U.S. and International Orders payable in U.S. Funds
Price is subject to change

Please make your cheque or money order payable to:

PARSTAR PUBLICATIONS

Suite 200   - or -   N.F. MPO Box 1902
309-2500 Barton Street East   Niagara Falls, NY
Hamilton, Ontario L8E 4A2   14302

For fundraising or volume purchases,
contact PARSTAR PUBLICATIONS for volume rates

Please allow 3-4 weeks for delivery

Name _____

Address _____

City _____ Province/State _____

Country_____ Postal code/Zip _____